How to Find Anything on the Internet for the Older Generation

Other "Older Generation" Titles

How to Find Anything on the Internet for the Older Generation

Robert Penfold

Bernard Babani (publishing) Ltd
The Grampians
Shepherds Bush Road
London W6 7NF
England
www.babanibooks.com

Please note

Although every care has been taken with the production of this book to ensure that any projects, designs, modifications, and/or programs, etc., contained herewith, operate in a correct and safe manner and also that any components specified are normally available in Great Britain, the Publisher and Author do not accept responsibility in any way for the failure (including fault in design) of any projects, design, modification, or program to work correctly or to cause damage to any equipment that it may be connected to or used in conjunction with, or in respect of any other damage or injury that may be caused, nor do the Publishers accept responsibility in any way for the failure to obtain specified components.

Notice is also given that if any equipment that is still under warranty is modified in any way or used or connected with home-built equipment then that warranty may be void.

© 2003 BERNARD BABANI (publishing) LTD

First published - October 2003
Reprinted - March 2004
Reprinted - November 2004
Reprinted - March 2005

British Library Cataloguing in Publication Data

A catalogue record for this book is available from the British Library

ISBN   0 85934 605 6

Cover Design by Gregor Arthur

Printed and bound in Great Britain by Cox and Wyman

Preface

The average age of Internet users has been rising in recent years. One reason for this is simply that the original young whiz kids of the Internet are now in their 30s. Another factor is that many in the 50 plus age group are discovering the joys of surfing. The range of information available on the Internet is now quite mind-boggling, and the number of pages passed the billion mark long ago. The Google search site claims to search well over three billion web pages. Having such a vast number of pages at your disposal is fine, but is does result in the slight problem of finding the one or two pages that contain the information that you require. Going through 3,300,000,000 pages one by one is not an option!

This book shows you how to use search engines to find what you are looking for quickly and efficiently without having to wade through hundreds or even thousands of irrelevant search results. It also deals with specialist searches for images, music, Internet radio and television stations, people, addresses, and postcodes. The final part of the book is a web guide divided into eight sections. These days the Internet has plenty of material that is of interest to the older generation, and the guide concentrates on the biggest and best sites that are of likely to be of particular interest to this age group.

Throughout, the text is kept as free from jargon as possible, and little computer expertise is assumed.

You do need to be able to get your PC online and know the basics of using it. If necessary, consult "The Internet for the older generation (BP600)" and (or) "Computing for the older generation (BP601)" and learn the basics first.

Thanks are due to the proprietors of the web sites featured in this book. I have not used any system of rating on the sites since they are all of a high standard. In a book such as this it is not possible to cover all the sites in a given category, so I have concentrated on those that have a lot to offer. No doubt there are many other really good sites out there, so the ones featured here should perhaps be considered good starting points rather than all the Internet has to offer.

Robert Penfold

Trademarks

Contents

2

Specialist searches 61

3

Just for us 157

4

Legal matters 181

5

6

7

8

Travel 251

9

News and weather 271

10

Genealogy 291

Things to note

Note that the http:// part of Internet addresses has mostly been omitted from the addresses provided in this book. This is simply because it is not normally needed when typing an Internet address into a browser. It will automatically add it ahead of what you type. A few Internet addresses are not of the usual www.name.com format, and with these the full address is given, including the http:// prefix. There should be no problems provided the addresses are used in the exact form shown here.

The Internet is not static, and web sites change from time to time. When you visit sites mentioned in this book the web pages might be slightly different to those shown herein. However, the information available and the facilities provided will probably remain much the same in most cases. The sites featured here are mostly of the mature variety, but even well established sites occasionally disappear or merge. In the fullness of time it is likely that a few will simply go or move to a different address. That is one of the "joys" of surfing. The vast majority of the sites should remain available at the specified addresses for many years though.

Web searching

Spiders

There are all sorts of ways in which people find web sites of interest to them. You can find a web site because someone tells you about it, because you see it advertised, or because it is recommended in a television program or a magazine article. In practice few people arrive at web sites via any of these routes. The vast majority of web site visits are the result of a web search or a link from another site. I suspect that many of the visits via links actually start with a web search and develop from some helpful results.

In order to get anywhere when surfing the Internet you need to master web searching. As we will see shortly, getting lots of results from one of the popular search sites, or "search engines" as they are called, is quite easy. The difficult part is in getting a few high quality results. Getting two or three million matches is very impressive, but are you really going to search through that lot for what you need? Learn how to get a few quality results from a search engine and the worldwide web is your oyster. You will find what you need in minutes or even seconds instead of spending hours wading through thousands of results.

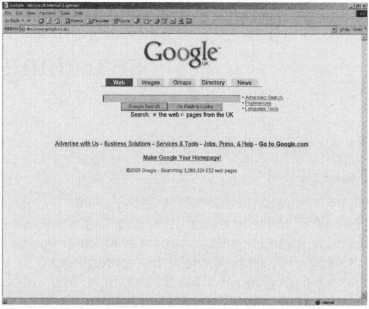

*Fig.1.1 The simple but effective Google.co.uk
        homepage*

What is a search engine and how does it work? A
search engine is basically just a computer that
contains details of the contents of millions of web
pages. In fact these days a big search engine has
details of more than a billion web pages. Because
the details are on the computer, it is possible to search
the pages very rapidly for the sort of information you
require. These days most web searches are
completed in a fraction of a second.

On the downside, no search engine contains details
of every web page. The search engines use automatic
systems to scan the web for details of each site that
is found. These devices are known by names such as

Fig.1.2 The textbox for the search string

"crawlers", "spiders", and "robots". They are very efficient, but they are fighting an uphill battle. The contents of the Internet are constantly changing, so no matter how good a spider might be, its search engine will never be bang up to date. Also, the "snapshots" of the pages might have incomplete details of the information on some of the pages. Despite these minor limitations, search engines will usually find what you are looking for, if it is there.

Searching

If you go to the homepage of a popular search engine you will invariably find a textbox somewhere on the page, and usually near the top. Figure 1.1 shows the homepage of the Google.co.uk site, and the textbox is, as expected, near the top of the page (Figure 1.2). Google was something of a latecomer to the Internet, and the other main search engines had a head start of many years. Its system sounds like something that might have been produced by Heath Robinson, with about ten thousand cheap PCs networked to produce one "mega" computer. The whole lot runs under the Linux operating system, which is essentially a piece of free software. While it might not sound like the recipe for the ultimate search engine, Google is extremely efficient and it soon established itself as the premier search engine. If you need to find things quickly on the Internet you will have to make Google your first port of call.

Returning to the textbox, this is where the search string is typed. In other words, this is where you type a word or list of words for the search engine to look for. If you type some characters but nothing appears in the textbox, left-clicking the mouse on the textbox should rectify matters. What the search engine will do is to look through every web page stored in its database in an attempt to find some that contain the word or words you have supplied.

Unless you tell it to do otherwise, Google will look for pages that contain all the words that you supply. Some other engines will look for any pages that contain at least one of the words. This second method provides more matches, but it is likely that most of the web pages found will be of no relevance to what you are looking for. If you are searching for something very unusual it is possible that there will be a problem in finding any matches at all. In most cases though, the problem is too many rather than too few matches, so it is best to start by searching for pages that contain all the words.

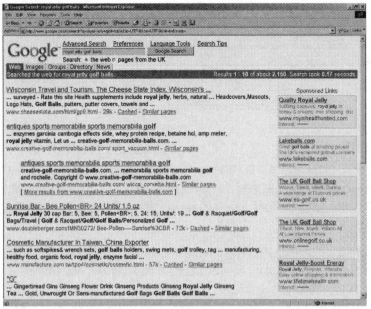

Fig.1.3 A large number of matches have been found

Well chosen words

The key to success with web searches is to use the right words in the search string. Suppose that you are a keen golfer, and someone has told you that it has been scientifically proven that polishing your balls with royal jelly will make them go ten percent further. In order to check for confirmation on the web there is no point in using "golf" as the search word, since there are certainly millions of pages that contain this word. Using "golf" and "balls" is unlikely to reduce the count very much. Similarly, "royal" and "jelly" probably occur on a huge number of pages. On the

Results **1 - 10** of about **2,150**. Search took **0.17** seconds.

*Fig.1.4 An amazing 2150 results have been found
          for the search string*

other hand, using all four words should greatly reduce the number of matches. On the face of it, royal jelly and golf-balls have nothing in common, so any pages that contain both should have the scientific research we require.

Since I made up this amazing piece of research, one might reasonably expect these four words to produce no matches. In fact they produced a substantial number of matches (Figure 1.3). The approximate number of matches is shown in the top right-hand corner of the page (Figure 1.4), and in this case it is about 2150.

Why are there so many results for a totally bogus search? One reason is simply the huge number of web pages currently on the Internet. There are so many pages containing so many combinations of words that there is a reasonable chance of any string of a few words producing some matches. Try putting a few random words into a search engine and see what it turns up. I tried "plasma", "goose", "fire", and "fan", and Google responded with about 1440 pages containing these four seemingly unrelated words.

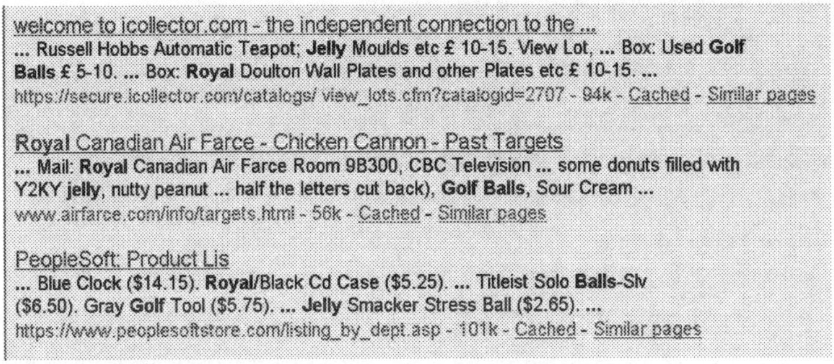

welcome to icollector.com - the independent connection to the ...
... Russell Hobbs Automatic Teapot; **Jelly** Moulds etc £ 10-15. View Lot, ... Box: Used **Golf**
Balls £ 5-10. ... Box: **Royal** Doulton Wall Plates and other Plates etc £ 10-15. ...
https://secure.icollector.com/catalogs/ view_lots.cfm?catalogid=2707 - 94k - Cached - Similar pages

Royal Canadian Air Farce - Chicken Cannon - Past Targets
... Mail: **Royal** Canadian Air Farce Room 9B300, CBC Television ... some donuts filled with
Y2KY **jelly**, nutty peanut ... half the letters cut back), **Golf Balls**, Sour Cream ...
www.airfarce.com/info/targets.html - 56k - Cached - Similar pages

PeopleSoft: Product Lis
... Blue Clock ($14.15). **Royal**/Black Cd Case ($5.25). ... Titleist Solo **Balls**-Slv
($6.50). Gray **Golf** Tool ($5.75). ... **Jelly** Smacker Stress Ball ($2.65). ...
https://www.peoplesoftstore.com/listing_by_dept.asp - 101k - Cached - Similar pages

Fig.1.5 The results from the search

Useful quotations

One reason that there were so many matches in the bogus research example was that the words "royal" and "jelly" tended to occur separately on pages. With a normal search it does not matter whether the search words occur together or well apart. The engine is looking for the right words on the page and will find a match either way.

Most search engines will place results higher in the list of results if the search words are close together, but this does not guarantee that the top results will all be relevant. Figure 1.5 shows three results from the bottom of the first page of results. Google helpfully shows brief snatches of text where it found the matches on the page. It can be seen from these the words "royal" and "jelly" are well separated.

Probably the most useful ploy for avoiding irrelevant results is to use quotation marks together with a short phrase. In this example royal jelly would be placed in double quotes ("royal jelly"), and a match would

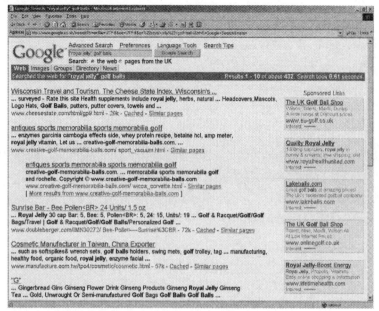

Fig.1.6 The result of the modified search

then be produced only if these two words occurred together and in the correct order. Note that search engines are not usually case-sensitive. In other words, a match is produced regardless of whether you use lower case or capital letters in the search string. For example, "royal", "Royal", and "ROYAL" would all match with "royal". These days this lack of case sensitivity is usually retained for search words within double quotation marks.

Figure 1.6 shows the result using the modified search string. Incredibly, there are still about 432 matching results! I suppose that with 432 results you could check through them all in a reasonable amount of time. The brief pieces of text shown for each page make it possible to sort out the pages of possible interest without having to open each one. Even using some form of high speed broadband Internet connection it can still take a long time to check even two or three dozen pages, so this feature is more than a little useful.

It is possible to reduce the number of matches still further by adding more words into the search string. For example, the words "further" and "percent" could be added to the search string. Using "percent" is a bit risky, because it could appear as a word or the percentage sign (%). Just adding "further" reduced the number of matches to a more manageable 32. Amazingly, adding the word "percent" still left eight matches, none of which were anything to do with my invented golfing tip. Placing "golf-balls" in double quotes still left three matches. It is an exaggeration to say that any selection of five or six words will produce results from a search engine, but clearly results can be produced from several seemingly unrelated words.

In this example some results were produced, but none covered the story we were interested in. This is not surprising since the story was a piece of pure invention, but there is actually a web site that carries the story. This is the spoof site that I placed on the Internet a couple of days before making the searches (Figure 1.7).

It did not show up in the search results because it had not been on the Internet long enough to be picked

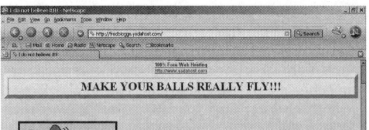

Fig.1.7 The spoof web page

up by a search engine. By the time you read this it might do so. This demonstrates the point that it is sometimes worth trying again at a later date if an initial search fails to produce any worthwhile results. Perhaps a new site will have been placed on the web during the gap, or an existing site might have been added into the databases of the search engines.

Punctuation

In the example search I used the totally separate words "golf" and "balls", but these two words are often hyphenated. Most search engines do not permit punctuation marks to be used in search strings, and will simply ignore them. Punctuation marks in web pages are usually treated as spaces. Therefore, as far as a search engine is concerned, there is no difference between "golf balls" and "golf-balls". On the other hand, neither of these will usually match with "golfballs". Mistakes are made in web pages, so you can sometimes get results using popular misspellings. These occur most frequently with the names of people and places (Davis instead of Davies for instance) and with the merging of hyphenated words.

It is perhaps worth mentioning that common words such as "the" and "and" will usually be ignored by search engines. Since they occur on practically every page written in the English language there is little point in including them in search strings. Of course, any words will be included in the search if they are part of a phrase placed in double quotation marks.

More is more

As we have already seen, when using Google it is possible to refine searches by adding more words into the search string. The more words you use, the fewer matches are likely to be found. Many users of search engines make the mistake of thinking that things work this way with all search engines. Unfortunately, each search engine has its own way of handling things and there is no guarantee that searches will work in strict Google fashion. In most cases there are major differences between the way Google and other engines process search strings.

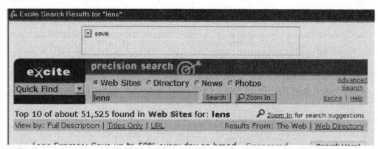

Fig.1.8 Over 51000 matches have been found

With many search engines adding more words into the search string does not reduce the number of matches, but actually has the opposite effect. Suppose you are a keen photographer in search of lens tests on the Internet. Figure 1.8 shows the result of using "lens" as the search string at the Excite.com search engine, while Figure 1.9 shows the result of adding "camera" and "test" to the string. A not inconsiderable 51000 or so matches in the first search have grown to over 1.3 million in the second!

So what has gone wrong? The Google search engine looks for pages that contain all the words you supply, but most search sites do not operate on this basis.

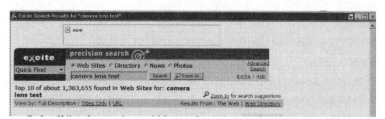

Fig.1.9 There are now over 1.3 million matches

Instead, any page that contains one of the words you supply will be considered a valid match. Hence the more words you supply in the search string, the greater the number of matches produced.

In the early days of the Internet the effectiveness of search engines tended to be rated by the number of results produced from a given search string. In those days there were relatively few sites, so finding any matches could be difficult. The Excite method ensured the greatest possible number of matches from a given search string, and it was the one that most search engines utilised at that time.

These days it is quality rather than quantity of results that is important, making the Google method the more practical one. However, search engines do enable users to control the way search strings are processed, so it is possible to refine searches by using more words.

In order to define things more accurately with most search engines you must add either a plus sign (+) or the word "AND" ahead of each word. This tells the search program that it must look for pages that contain all the words and not just one of them. Repeating the search with the plus signs added reduces the number of matches to just 715 (Figure 1.10).

Omitting the plus signs is a common mistake, and many users end up using single word search strings in an attempt to keep the number of matches within reason. Using several words and the plus signs is

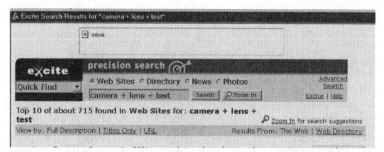

Fig.1.10 Now a more manageable 715 matches

clearly a much more effective way of searching the Internet. The number of matches is kept within reason and you tend to home in on a higher percentage of relevant sites.

Less is less

There is another useful trick that can help to remove matches that are of no real use. Suppose that in the lens test example you are only interested in sites that provide test results, but most of the sites suggested by the search engine have titles like "How to Test Your Camera Lens" and do not provide any lens tests. It is difficult to remove this type of site from the results by using more search words, since words in this type of site are likely to crop up in the sites of interest as well. The alternative method is to give the search program a word or words that can be used to eliminate pages from the results. In this case the word "how" could be used as the filter, with any page containing this word being removed from the list of matches.

Fig.1.11 This time there are just 190 results

A minus sign (-) or sometimes the word "NOT" is used in front of a word to indicate to the search engine that you are looking for pages that do not contain that word. Figure 1.11 shows the result of the lens test search using this refinement, and the number of matches has now been reduced to a very much more manageable figure of about 190. Obviously this method does risk filtering out relevant pages that just happen to have the word you are avoiding. This method is especially risky with a general word such as "how", which can occur in just about any page about any subject.

If you can find a suitable word or words it is a method that will often provide good results. In this example there were probably a substantial number of relevant pages that were eliminated from the search result, but there were still plenty of pages remaining. Also, these pages contained a high percentage that was relevant, rather than just the odd page here and there

Fig.1.12 The options at the Excite search site

that was of interest. It is certainly worth trying in cases where adding words to the search string fails to focus the search more tightly.

UK and Ireland

Most search engines have a range of advanced options to help reduce the number of irrelevant pages still further. If you are only interested in UK sites and companies it is a good idea to go to the UK version of the search engine. Most of the large search companies have a general or US site with a .com address, plus other sites for specific countries.

One of these is usually a UK web site having a .co.uk address. Figure 1.12 shows the options available at the Excite.co.uk site. The three radio buttons beneath the textbox enable the search to be restricted to the sites in the UK, or sites in Ireland. Of course, a full search of the Web is available as well.

The UK version of the Yahoo site offers similar facilities (Figure 1.13). The radio buttons enable the search to be restricted to the UK or Ireland, or the whole of Yahoo can be searched. Radio buttons

Fig.1.13 Yahoo! provides similar options

operate like the waveband buttons on a radio, and if you select one you automatically deselect whatever button was selected previously. Consequently, if you wish to search for sites in the UK and in Ireland it must be done using separate searches.

If you are looking for (say) a shop in the UK that sells lawnmower spare parts, by restricting the search to the UK it is possible to immediately filter out a vast number of sites that will be of no interest to you. The difference made by this type of filtering is usually vast. The number of matches will usually be reduced by well over 90 percent.

These systems are less than perfect though. Apparently they operate by searching web servers located in the UK or Ireland, as appropriate. The nature of the Internet is such that UK and Irish sites can be hosted elsewhere in the world. Similarly, sites from elsewhere can be hosted in the UK and Ireland. In practice this feature usually works quite well though.

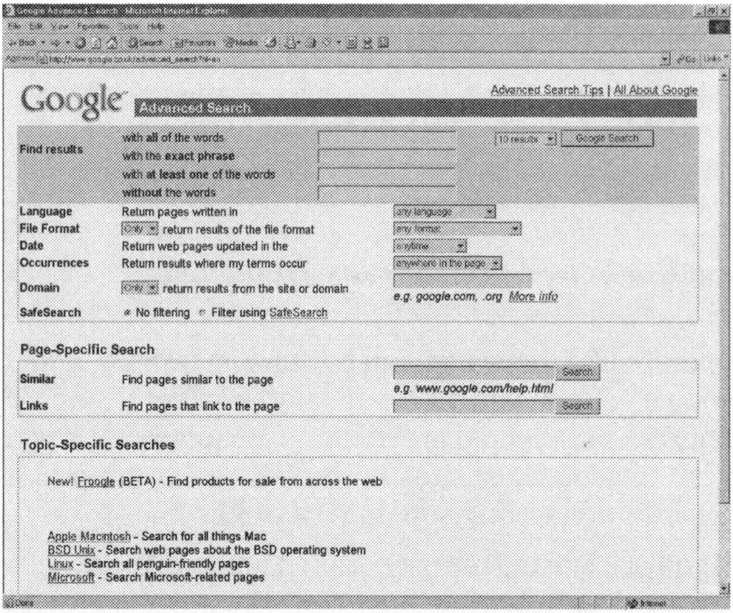

Fig.1.14 Google's advanced search facility

Advanced

Some sites have a button that is operated in order to go into a special page that handles advanced searching. Figure 1.14 shows the advanced search facilities of the Google.co.uk search engine. Amongst other things this enables a search to be made for specified words, pages containing certain words to be filtered, and pages not in the specified language to be filtered. In general, it is a lot easier to use the advanced search than it is to add plus signs, etc., into the search string. Also, there might be facilities in the advanced search page that are not available by other means.

The advanced search pages are usually quite easy to use. In the case of Google, the "with all the words" field is the usual Google search string. Only web pages that contain all these words will be included in the list of results. The "with the exact phrase" field gives a feature that is the equivalent of placing words within double quotation marks. A match will only be produced with web pages that include the phrase used here. If you need to include two or three phrases, place each one within double quotes.

You have to be careful when using the "with at least one of the words" field. Any web pages that include at least one of the words used here will be included in the results. Only unusual words, type numbers, and the like should be used here. Using any common words will produce at least several million matches. Note that you can obtain this type of search with a normal Google search string by using "OR" in front of words. Using the "without the words" field is like using a minus sign or NOT in front of a word in a search string. Any pages that contain the supplied word or words will be filtered from the list of results.

With some searches you tend to find that most of the pages in the search results are in the wrong language. This is most likely to occur when using proper names, which are not normally translated into another language. For example, on a French or German web site, Tony Blair will still be called Tony Blair. The Language menu (Figure 1.15) enables the search to be restricted to pages written in a particular language, and English is, of course, one of the options. Although

Language	Return pages written in	any language ▾
File Format	Only ▾ return results of the file format	Croatian
		Czech
Date	Return web pages updated in the	Danish
		Dutch
Occurrences	Return results where my terms occur	English
		Estonian
Domain	Only ▾ return results from the site or domain	Finnish
		French
SafeSearch	⊙ No filtering ○ Filter using SafeSearch	German
		Greek
		Hebrew

Fig.1.15 The search can be limited to one language

this feature does not seem to be 100 percent reliable, it will certainly remove the vast majority of pages that are in the wrong language.

Red-faced matches

It is worth looking at the other advanced search features, but they are mostly of limited use in general searches. However, the SafeSearch feature is one you might find useful. Most search engines will happily track down whatever material is required, including pages that are pornographic or sexual in nature. Unfortunately, even quite innocent search strings can sometimes produce matches with sites that have a strong sexual content.

When searching for web sites supporting the Flash MX graphics program I was not surprised that some of the matches were for sites having photographs of streakers in action. It was more surprising when a search for information on a graphics tablet called a Pen Partner produced a number of matches for pages giving details of a sex aid!

This can all be a bit unfortunate if you are showing children or the vicar's wife how to search the Web,

SafeSearch	No filtering	Filter using SafeSearch

Fig.1.16 The SafeSearch filtering is optional

and search for cheesecake recipes provides matches with some hardcore pornography sites. However, it is a problem that is easily avoided, since most search engines have a facility that tries to filter out matches with pages that have a strong sexual content. In the case of Google's Advanced Search page there are two radio buttons which permit the SafeSearch adult filtering system to be turned on and off (Figure 1.16).

If you look for similar facilities on other search engines you might find them, but adult filtering is by no means as common as it used to be. You may have to do some delving in order to unearth any filtering options that are available. A feature of this type is available from the Lycos engine if you go to the advanced search page (Figure 1.17). If an advanced search facility is available, it is probably the best place to look. Where appropriate, only use a search engine that does have these facilities.

It is only fair to point out that no adult filtering system can be guaranteed to be 100 percent effective, but a system of this type should filter the vast majority of

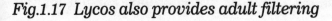

BLOCK OFFENSIVE CONTENT	Strict- Filter explicit content Moderate (default setting) - Intelligent adult content reduction. Off - Do not filter explicit content.	Reduce amount of explicit content in my search results

Fig.1.17 Lycos also provides adult filtering

potentially embarrassing search results. There is also a slight risk that this type of filtering will remove useful links. These systems operate by looking for "naughty" words in the scanned pages, and in some cases a page will be filtered if it contains a word that in turn contains a "naughty" word, even if the whole word is totally inoffensive. Some words can be "naughty" or inoffensive depending on the context. With a search for Mary Poppins you might find pages containing the name Dick Van Dyke were filtered out! However, the number of suitable matches removed by adult filtering is usually very small.

Wildcards

Sometimes there can be search problems due to different spellings being used for the same thing or the same person. For example, names in Russian and many other languages are given their western spellings by converting them phonetically. In other words, the spelling is one that reflects the sound of the original name. The problem with this method is that the same name can be converted in two or more different ways, giving rise to alternative spellings for the same name.

The Russian composer Tchaikovsky is also known in the west as Tchaikowsky for example. I have seen other versions such as Tchaikowski. There can also be difficulties due to differences between American English and what for the lack of a better term we will call English English. For example, looking for the

"XYZ Centre" will not produce a match for the "XYZ Center".

Some search engines allow the use of wildcards, and these will often permit a single search to accommodate two different spellings. This feature is not as common as it used to be, but AltaVista permits the asterisk (*) to be used as a wildcard. A match will then be produced with any letter at that position in the word. For example, "Tchaiko*sky" will match both "Tchaikovsky" and "Tchaikowsky", and "Cent**" will match both "Centre" and "Center".

Too much

Even with careful selection of the search string you may find that the search engines tend to produce large numbers of matches. There is no getting away from the fact that the Web contains massive amounts of information, with more pages being added every day. Particularly if you are searching for information on a popular subject, there could be many thousands of pages that are relevant to your search criteria. It could be that most of these contain the information you require, but it is likely that many will barely touch on your subject of interest. With the web still expanding, it is a problem that is likely to get even worse over the next few years.

The search engines try to rate pages in order of likely interest, and sometimes provide each one with a score that indicates its likely relevance to your search criteria. Some advocate looking only at the first few

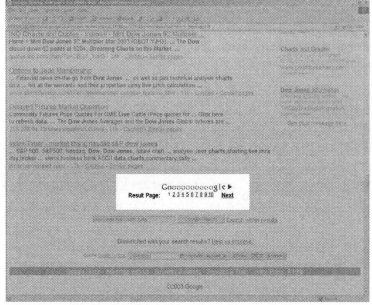

Fig.1.18 The list of pages of search results

pages of matches, and then trying again with a new search strategy if useful results are not obtained. I have often found it useful to dive into the middle of the list, or even have a look at matches near the bottom of the list that have very lowly scores. The search engines are based on some very clever programming techniques, but they can not mind-read. The search engine's rating system might have totally misjudged the type of thing you are after. There might just be some useful pages listed in the middle or even at the bottom of the list.

Google provides a numbered list of search result pages near the bottom of each page (Figures 1.18 and

1.19).   Using
this you can go
to the next page
or jump to one
of the others
simply by left-

Fig.1.19 A close-up of the list

clicking the appropriate number in the list. When
there are a lot of results you can delve deep into the
results by clicking the highest number, then the
highest number on the new page that appears, and
so on. Most search engines use essentially the same
system.

Missing pages

One of the most frustrating search problems is when
you locate what looks like a very promising page using
a search engine, but linking to that page produces
some sort of error message rather than the page. You
soon become familiar with the dreaded "404" error
message which means that the page can not be found.
There is a similar problem where the page appears,
but it does not seem to have anything to do with the
subject you are researching.

When searching the Internet it is useful to bear in
mind the general way in which the search engines
function. Many seem to believe that the Web is
scanned for suitable matches each time a search is
made. As pointed out previously, it does not work in
this fashion, and this approach would take far too long.
Instead, the search engines scan the Web and place

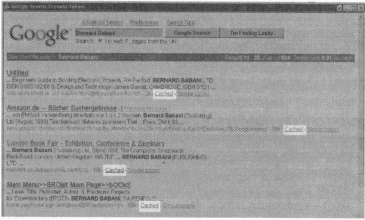

Fig.1.20 Google usually provides a Cached option

so-called "snapshots" of each page into a huge database. Each time a search is carried out it is the pages in this database that are scanned and not the real thing on the Internet.

This method enables a massive number of pages to be searched in what is usually a fraction of a second, but it is "second-hand" data that is being scanned. Web pages are deleted or altered from time to time, and this can produce discrepancies between the content of the database and the actual pages available on the Internet. An error message could indicate that the page has been deleted, or it could just be that the server has gone down. It could also be due to a problem on the route between your computer and the target web site. Try operating the browser's Refresh button, and repeat this once or twice if necessary. If the page still fails to load, make a note of the web address and try again later.

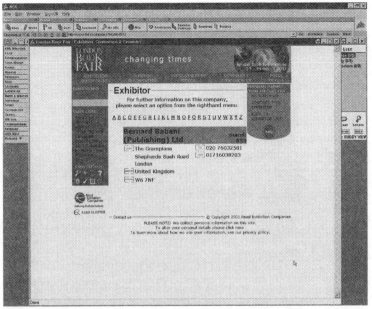

Fig.1.21 The real web page, not a cached one

Where a page has been changed or deleted it might be possible to obtain some of the information it contained. In some cases it is possible to download the "snapshot" stored on the server, but bear in mind that this is usually an abbreviated version of the page. Figure 1.20 shows a section of some search results obtained using the Google.co.uk search engine, and for most of the entries there is a Cached option. Selecting this option results in the snapshot of the page being displayed, rather than the page being downloaded from the actual web site.

Figure 1.21 shows the "real thing", while Figure 1.22 shows the cached version of the same page. In

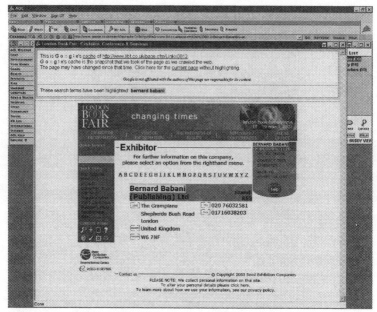

Fig.1.22 The cached version of the page

general, the text from the original page will be totally
or largely intact in the cached version, but any major
graphic content is almost certain to be omitted as it
is of no help when conducting searches. Provided it
is the words you are after, which will usually be the
case, the cached page should be as good as the
original.

Cut short

Another useful ploy is to try using a shortened version
of the web address provided by the search engine.
Suppose that the address is:

www.thebestcamerawebsite.com/cameras/lenses/
autofocus/tests

Even if this page no longer exists, the web site that used to contain it is still likely to be in business, and it might still contain useful information. One approach is to go to the home page web address, which is "www.thebestcamerasite.com" in this example. From here you might be able to follow links that lead to something useful, either on this site or another one.

An alternative approach is to try the address with the last section removed, which means leaving out the "/tests" in this example. If this is not successful, remove another section, which would be "/autofocus" in this case. Once you are into the site, look for links that will take you to something useful. These methods will not work in every case, but they often produce something helpful.

Missing links

A common mistake when looking through pages suggested by a search engine is to look only at the main content and ignore everything else. If a site covers the right subject area but does not have the exact information you require, it could still be useful. Many sites have some form of bulletin board facility where users can post information and ask questions. If the information you require is proving elusive it might be worthwhile posting a question to see if anyone can come up with the right answers. Requests for information often result in someone providing either the required information or a site that tells you what you need to know.

The most important thing to look for on "near miss" sites is a list of links to similar sites. Web sites often contain links to other sites of a similar nature, usually with a brief description of each one. These sites in turn will probably have links to yet more sites of possible interest. Having found a "near miss" site the best tactic is probably to follow the links from site to site, rather than going back to the search engine's list of pages, most of which are probably irrelevant. There is no guarantee of success when following links, but some real gems can be turned up in this way.

Blank results

As already pointed out, the usual problem when searching the Internet is too many matches rather than too few. You will not always find a plethora of matches though. This is something where you have to be realistic in your expectations. Although there is a massive amount of information available on the Internet, there is no guarantee that you will always be able to locate the information you require. The more obscure the subject, the lower the chances of success.

If you draw a blank using one search engine, try another or even several more if necessary. I sometimes have to search for technical information about computing and electronics. It is quite normal for the first, one, two, or even three search engines to produce nothing useful, before I finally "come up trumps". As explained in the next section, there are ways of searching several sites simultaneously, and this approach is worthwhile if you are searching for something quite obscure and difficult to find.

A complete lack of response is often due to a spelling error. Remember that only an exact match will do when using double quotation marks. In a similar vein, if you are looking for pages that contain all the specified search words, a spelling error in one of the words will be sufficient to prevent any matches from being obtained.

Particularly when dealing with names, double-check that you are spelling everything correctly. The same applies if you obtain numerous matches that are nothing to do with the subject matter you are seeking, or a lot of the sites are in a foreign language. The misspelled word might not mean anything in English, but it could be quite common in (say) German or Polish.

Turbo search

If you need to search regularly for hard to find information on the Web it can be very time consuming going from one search engine to another trying to find elusive snippets of information. One solution to the problem is to use software that takes the provided search criteria and then uses it to search for results on a number of search engines. It then shows the consolidated results. The results do not pop up almost

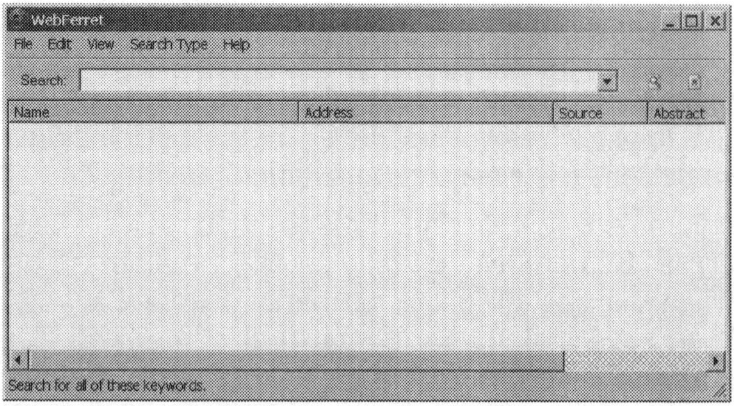

Fig.1.23 The WebFerret main window

instantly in the same way that they do when utilising a single search engine, but the process is still very much faster than the manual approach.

WebFerret is one of the best known programs of this type, and there is a trial version that can be obtained from the larger software download sites or from www.ferretsoft.com. Figure 1.23 shows the main window where the search string is entered in the Search textbox. The usual search options are available, such as searching for matches for any

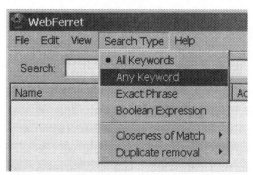

Fig.1.24 The search options

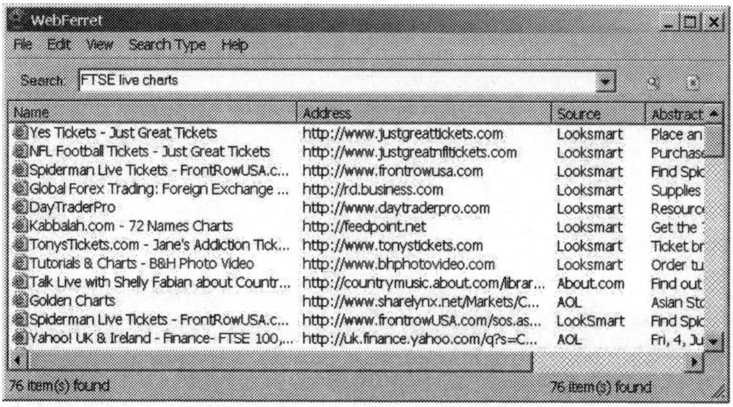

Fig.1.25 The search results in the main panel

keyword or all the keywords. The required type of search is selected from the Search menu (Figure 1.24).

Four options are available in the Duplicate Removal submenu, but it is advisable to use the default setting, which removes duplicate URLs (web addresses). Multiple matches for pages is a common problem when using search engines. It occurs where there are several places in a page that provide a match for the search criteria. Most search engines list a match for each occurrence of the search string in a page, and this is one of the reasons that so many matches are often produced. When using software that provides the search by way of several search engines the problem is multiplied. Having duplicated URLs filtered out helps to keep things manageable.

Once everything has been set up correctly the Start button just to the right of the textbox is operated and

1 Web searching

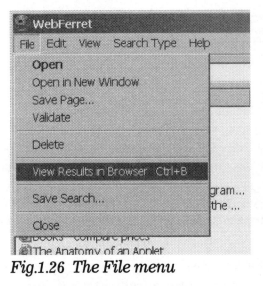

the searching begins. The results are displayed in the lower section of the window (Figure 1.25). Double-clicking on one of the entries in the list results in the corresponding web page being

Fig.1.26 The File menu

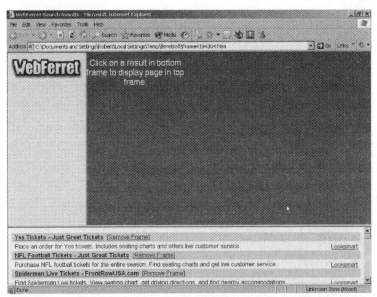

Fig.1.27 The window is split into two sections

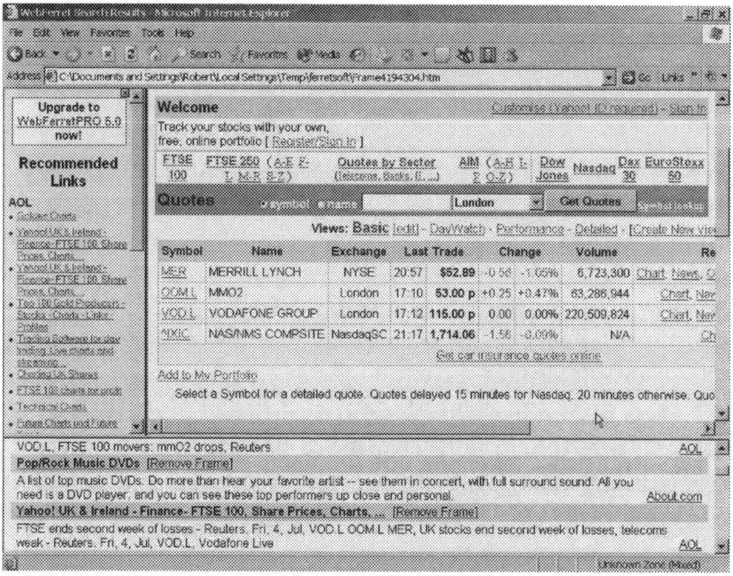

Fig.1.28 Pages are displayed in the upper frame

displayed in the default browser. Unless you have installed a different one as the default, Windows will use Internet Explorer.

An alternative way of viewing pages is to select View Results in Browser from the File menu (Figure 1.26). This will again launch the default browser. However, this time the browser window is split into two main sections (Figure 1.27). The larger (upper) window is used to show the web pages selected from the list of matches in the lower section. Left-click a link in the lower frame and the corresponding page will be displayed in the upper frame (Figure 1.28).

If a large number of matches are being produced or the search is taking a long time, operating the Stop button (just to the right of the Start button) brings

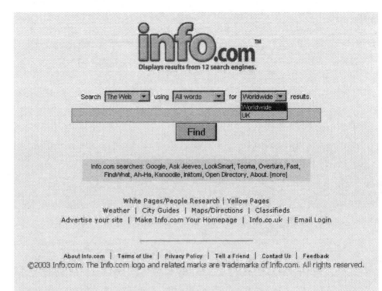

Fig.1.29 The search can be refined

the process to a halt. Programs such as Web Ferret are very impressive in use, and are of real benefit if you mostly search for obscure information that is normally time-consuming to track down. These programs are not really of much use when searching for material that is on the Web in abundance. Using one search engine will usually provide masses of matches, which usually makes it pointless to use several search engines at once. You simply multiply the information overload problem.

Meta search

Some search sites now offer an alternative to software like WebFerret by providing essentially the same

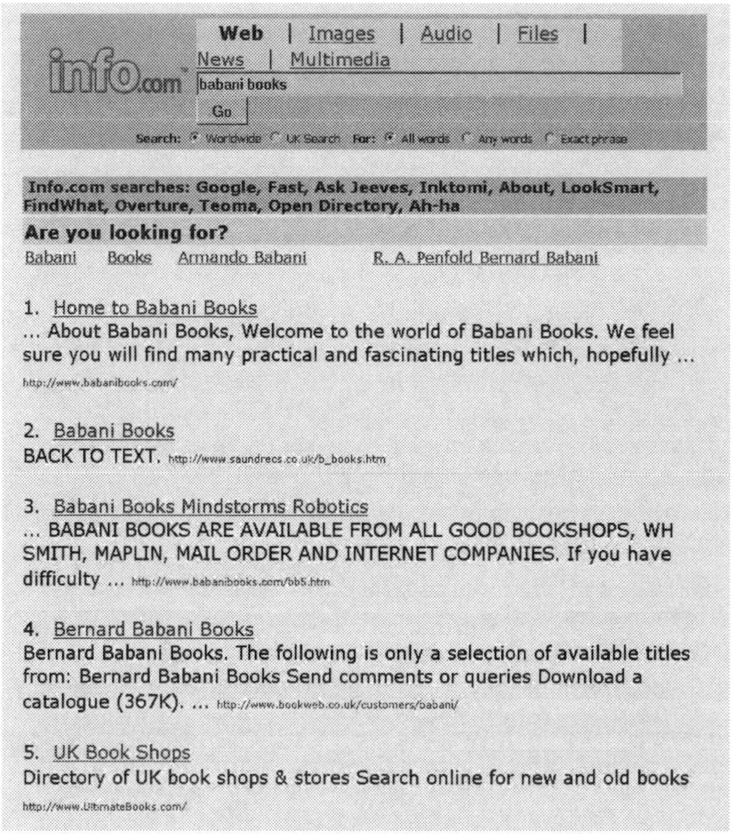

Web | Images | Audio | Files |
News | Multimedia
babani books
Go
Search: ⊙ Worldwide ○ UK Search For: ⊙ All words ○ Any words ○ Exact phrase

Info.com searches: Google, Fast, Ask Jeeves, Inktomi, About, LookSmart, FindWhat, Overture, Teoma, Open Directory, Ah-ha

Are you looking for?

Babani   Books   Armando Babani   R. A. Penfold Bernard Babani

1. Home to Babani Books
... About Babani Books, Welcome to the world of Babani Books. We feel sure you will find many practical and fascinating titles which, hopefully ...
http://www.babanibooks.com/

2. Babani Books
BACK TO TEXT. http://www.saundrecs.co.uk/b_books.htm

3. Babani Books Mindstorms Robotics
... BABANI BOOKS ARE AVAILABLE FROM ALL GOOD BOOKSHOPS, WH SMITH, MAPLIN, MAIL ORDER AND INTERNET COMPANIES. If you have difficulty ... http://www.babanibooks.com/bb5.htm

4. Bernard Babani Books
Bernard Babani Books. The following is only a selection of available titles from: Bernard Babani Books Send comments or queries Download a catalogue (367K). ... http://www.bookweb.co.uk/customers/babani/

5. UK Book Shops
Directory of UK book shops & stores Search online for new and old books
http://www.UltimateBooks.com/

Fig.1.30 The search results from Info.com

facility. These are known as meta search sites, and they typically search using about 12 search engines. Info.com is an example of a meta search engine, and it is used much like any other search engine. Menus at the top of the page provide the usual facilities for refining the search (Figure 1.29). Searching for "Babani" and "books" produced a normal list of

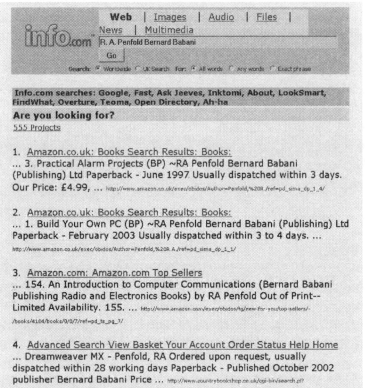

Fig.1.31 Themed results are available

results (Figure 1.30), but the results were drawn from 12 different search engines, including the all-important Google.

It is increasingly common for search engines to analyse the results and look for common themes, and it is more or less a standard feature of meta search engines. In this case four common themes are listed

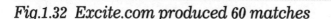

Meta-Search results for "application output steps hidden Aardvark" (1 - 20 of 60)   page: **1** - 2 - 3 - next

Fig.1.32 Excite.com produced 60 matches

in the "Are you looking for" section just above the
search results. It is gratifying to see that I merit my
own section! This is a useful feature if one of the
suggested themes matches your requirements. Just
left-click the appropriate link and a list of matches
will be displayed (Figure 1.31). The filtered results
should contain a high percentage that are relevant
to your search and relatively few that are of no
interest.

As a test of how well (or otherwise) meta search
engines work I used five words chosen at random
(application, output, steps, hidden, and aardvark), and
used them in searches for pages that contained all
five words. Info.com produced 60 results, as did

Fig.1.33 Google produced some 118 matches

Excite.com (Figure 1.32), which these days is a meta
search engine that uses Google and eight other
engines. Strangely, the same search string produced
118 matches when used with Google and the same
search criteria (Figure 1.33).

So why would a multiple search produce fewer results? The most likely explanation is that meta search engines, by necessity, have to be good at pruning duplicate entries for web pages, and might even filter duplicate entries for the same site. Although Google seems to be producing nearly twice as many matches, the Google results almost certainly contained a significant amount of duplication. The results from a meta search engine are therefore more focussed, and could contain a few additional matches. A large search engine such as Google is so efficient it would be naïve to expect additional searches from other engines to produce a large increase in the number of results.

Shortcut

Many people make the mistake of using search engines when there is no real need to do so. If there is an obvious source of information always try that source first. For example, suppose you required some information on a Channel 4 program. You could use a search engine to find sites that cover that program, and you would probably find what you need before too long. On the other hand, you could simply go to the Channel 4 web site to look for information. There is a good chance of finding the information you require straight away, or failing that you may find a useful link to another site. Try the obvious sites first and only resort to a search engine if it is really necessary to do so.

Search anyway

Very occasionally the opposite approach can be useful. Suppose you know the correct web address but you are not getting through to the site. Trying to access the site by first locating it using a search engine and then using the search engine's link is sometimes successful. One reason this will sometimes work is that the web site has moved, and the search engine is linking to the new address. Most web sites have a message on the old web site giving directions to the new one, or simply use some form of automatic redirection. Not all relocated sites have these facilities though, and they are unlikely to be maintained for long once a site has moved.

Another reason that this method can work is that it takes you to the site via a different route. This route might bypass a blockage that is troubling the original route to the site. The Internet has far more sites and users than a few years ago, but it is actually far more reliable than it was back then. It is not perfect though, and probably never will be. Sites can and do go offline from time to time, either due to a fault or for maintenance. If you can not get through to a site it is worth trying later in the day, or if that fails try a day or two later.

It can sometimes be frustrating when you find a site that looks promising, but it lacks the information you require because the site is incomplete. Signs saying "Site under construction", often complete with an animated workman character, used to be found on a fair percentage of sites. It became a bit of a bad joke with surfers, and it is a practice that has largely died out. If you find a promising but incomplete site it is certainly worth checking back occasionally to see if it has been expanded or even completed. However, experience suggests that sites published while they are still under construction are only rarely completed. They are far more likely to suddenly disappear without trace.

Easy searching

If you have real difficulty getting to grips with OR, NOT, etc., and nearly always end up with huge numbers of irrelevant matches, one option is to use an advanced search facility where you just fill in a form and operate the Search button. This approach was covered previously. An interesting alternative is to use one of the modern search engines that try to make things easier. These are known as "natural language" search engines, because you ask them a question using the same wording that you would use to ask a person the same question.

One of the best known of these is AskJeeves.co.uk (which is also at ask.com), and this is the one that will be used for this example. I recently needed to know what a purchase order is. This is a good example of the type of thing that can be difficult to find using a normal search engine even if you are pretty expert at these things. The individual words "purchase" and "order" are likely to appear in a vast number of web pages. Putting them together within double quotation marks reduces the number of

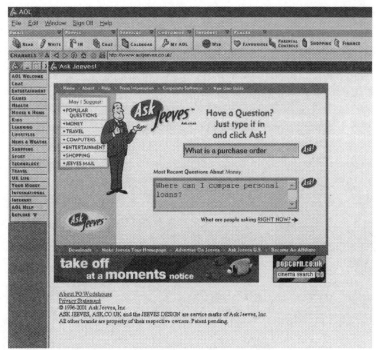

Fig.1.34 First, ask "Jeeves" a question

matches, but tends to give numerous results about accounting software that are of no help at all.

With a natural language search engine such as AskJeeves.co.uk you simply type in a question as if you were asking a person for help, so I simply asked, "What is a purchase order" (Figure 1.34). The search engine analyses the phrase that you have typed in an attempt to find keywords that will help it to understand what you require. In most cases it will find more than one line of enquiry, and it will then give a list of alternatives in an attempt to narrow down the search.

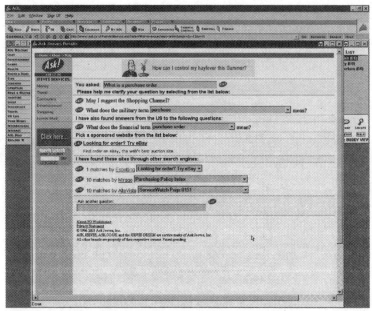

Fig.1.35 The initial results from "Jeeves"

The initial result of this search is shown in Figure 1.35, and one of the things on offer is a definition of the financial term "purchase order". This is clearly what I required, and it linked to the definition I was seeking (Figure 1.36). There is no guarantee that this sort of instant result will always be produced, but a search engine of this type is well worth trying, particularly if you have problems with conventional search engines. Note that the AskJeeves.co.uk site is undergoing a few changes, so by the time you read this the site might look a bit different to the illustrations shown here. It will still be used in essentially the same way though.

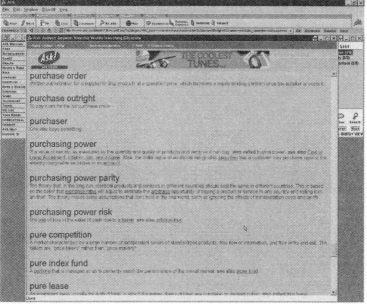

Fig.1.36 The answer has been found

Sponsored results

When using search engines you will probably notice that you often get rather more than the search results. Most engines produce a certain amount of advertising that is related to the words in the search string. At one time the sponsored results were mixed in with the ordinary results and were usually placed well to the fore. Google has always kept the sponsored results well separated from the normal output of its search engine, and other companies are starting to follow a similar policy.

The sponsored links on a Google results page are in the form of one or two banners just above the normal

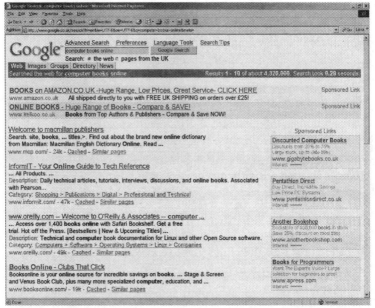

Fig.1.37 The sponsored links are clearly labelled

results, and small panels just to the right of them
(Figure 1.37). They are clearly marked "Sponsored
Links", so no one should be misled into thinking that
these are standard search results. You can simply
ignore the sponsored results, and with many searches
they will be of little or no relevance to what you are
seeking. However, if you are looking for goods or
services on the Internet it is likely that some of these
links will lead to something useful. It is certainly
worth quickly scanning through them to see if there
is anything that looks promising. Unfortunately, many
of these links are for companies in the USA, but there
is often a useful selection of links to UK companies.

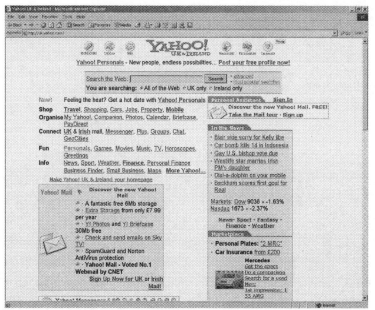

Fig.1.38 Yahoo!'s search facilty

Directory

Many surfers tend to get confused about the difference between Internet directories and search engines. The situation is blurred by the fact that some sites offer both facilities. Google has search facilities, but not much else is on offer. These days there is actually a Directory option on the homepage, and it is likely that in due course this will expand to rival the major Internet directories. At the moment, Google is primarily a search engine rather than a directory.

Yahoo! tends to be regarded by many as a search engine, and it does have a search facility. However,

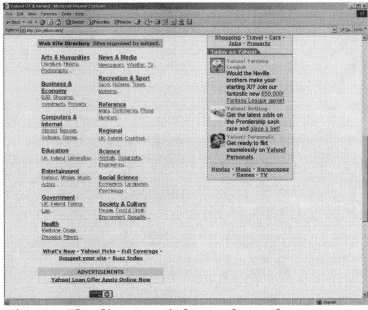

Fig.1.39 The directory is lower down the page

the search facility makes use of Google's technology, and as things stand it is a tiny part of a huge site. Yahoo! is primarily an Internet directory and general information site. A site of this type is sometimes called a portal, as it is used as a means of entering other sites on the Internet.

Like many of the big Internet companies, Yahoo! has a main site (Yahoo.com) which is primarily for people in the USA, plus numerous additional sites for other countries. The site for the UK and Ireland is Yahoo.co.uk, and in general it is better to use the site for your particular country. On entering the Yahoo! site the upper part of the homepage is used to access

Fig.1.40 Various types of review are available

the search facilities and general information, such as the financial section of the site (Figure 1.38). The directory is lower down on the page (Figure 1.39) where various categories and subcategories are listed.

Suppose that you have seen a HP 1220C inkjet printer at a good price in a sale, and you would like one or two reviews to see if it is a good buy. One of the categories in the directory is "Computers and Internet", and this has "Reviews" as a subcategory. Left-clicking this link produces another page, and this one has "Printers" listed in the Additional Categories (Figure 1.40). This looks promising, and operating

Fig.1.41 Still further options are offered

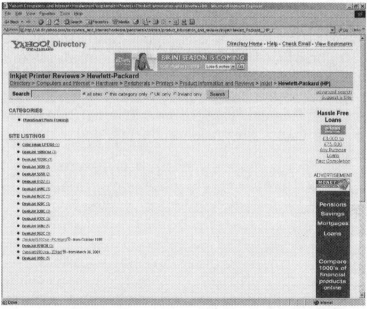

Fig.1.42 There is a link for HP printers

the link produces another page that includes further links (Figure 1.41). The "Buyers Guides" link might provide some useful background information, but for something more specific the "Inkjet" link looks more worthwhile.

This produces more choices (Figure 1.42), with a list of printer manufacturers that includes HP. Operating this link produces a list of HP inkjet printers down

Fig,1.43 There are reviews for several HP printers

the left-hand side of the page (Figure 1.43), and the 1220C printer is included in the list. Activating this link produces a page that

Fig.1.44 Success at last

contains two links to reviews (Figure 1.44). These links each lead to a review of the HP 1220C printer, and Figure 1.45 shows the PCWORLD.COM review.

If you require the right type of information, then the directory approach will often find what you require. The number of web pages included in a directory is relatively small though, so it is unlikely to be of much

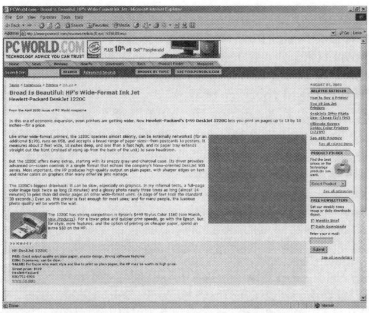

Fig.1.45 The review from US PC World site

use when looking for information on topics that are not popular.   Also, as this example amply demonstrated, you often have to delve quite deeply into a directory's structure before you unearth the required pages. The pages of directories are often very "busy" and arranged in a slightly confusing fashion. It is easy to get sidetracked into a "blind ally". A search engine will often find the same information quicker. One advantage of the directory approach is that it makes it easy to explore a general topic. In this example, having found the printer reviews it would be easy to find reviews of rival printers.

Finally

Search engines have facilities that enable you to produce better focussed searches that produce a high proportion of relevant results. You will need to use these in order to optimise your searches, but do not lose sight of the fact that it is primarily the search string that determines the quality of search results. Giving some thought to the search string will provide much better results than simply typing the first few words that spring to mind.

As an example of determining a good search string, I recently entered a competition where you had to answer three questions. One of these was "what is the name of the mountain near Rio De Janeiro on which the famous statue of Christ is situated?" An Internet search engine is ideal for tracking down this type of information, and with a suitable search string

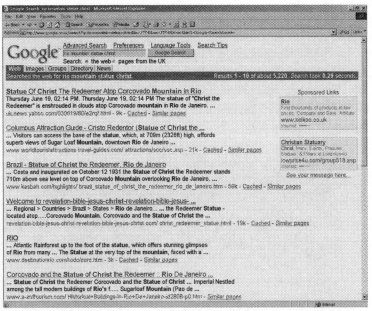

Fig.1.46 The answer is in the search results page

it should take a matter of seconds. It is just a matter of stripping out the ordinary words and leaving the important ones. The important words are "mountain", "Rio", "statue", and "Christ".

Using this search string in Google produced the result shown in Figure 1.46. There is no need to go into any of these pages, since the first entry provides the answer. The statue stands on Corcovado Mountain. As a point of interest, the first page listed not only provides the answer to the question, but it even provides a nice photograph of the statue (Figure 1.47). The second page in the list provides tourist information and information about the history of the

Thursday June 19, 02:14 PM

The statue of "Christ the Redeemer" is enshrouded in clouds atop Corcovado mountain in Rio de Janeiro. Rio has been named as the friendliest city in the world despite being crowded and dangerous. REUTERS/ Gregg Newton

Fig.1.47 More information and a photograph

statue. Within reason, whatever you wanted to know about the statue could probably be located within a minute or so.

If you find it difficult to pick out the key words it is worth trying a natural language search engine. To a large extent these engines work by stripping out all

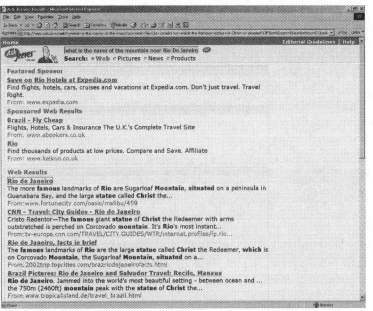

Fig.1.48 "Jeeves" has also found the answer

the common words and then using the remaining words in a conventional search. They usually work very well with something like this competition question. Using the full question in the Ask Jeeves search engine produced the result shown in Figure 1.48. This time the answer is in the second entry, and as before, the first two or three pages in the list provide photographs and lots of information about the statue.

Try to get the spelling right, and check it carefully if you get some odd looking results that seem to have little to do with your search words. Some search engines, including Google, actually look for possible

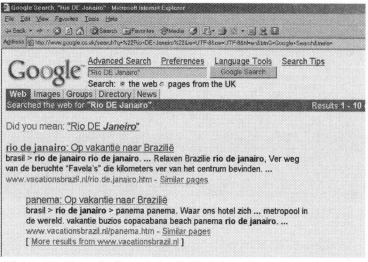

Fig.1.49 Google has queried the incorrect spelling

errors in your search words and will sometimes enquire whether you meant to type "xyz" instead of "zxy". In Figure 1.49 I deliberately type "Rio De Janairo" instead of "Rio De Janeiro". The Google search engine has duly spotted a likely error and asked if I meant "Rio De Janeiro".

Sometimes the search string will actually be correct. Proper names for example, can fool the engine into thinking that you have made an error. Simply ignore the suggestion if this occurs. If the suggested spelling is correct, just left-click on it and the search will be repeated using the correct spelling (Figure 1.50).

Make good use of double quotation marks. Again for a competition, I needed to know the name of the

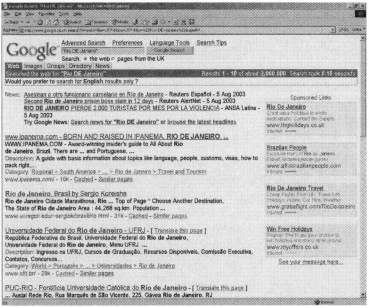

Fig.1.50 The search with the right spelling

person who came up with the famous "Wagner's music is better than it sounds" quotation. I knew that it was not, as often stated, Mark Twain, but another American writer of the same period. Unfortunately, I could not remember the name.

Using "Wagner" and "better than it sounds" (complete with the double quotation marks) as the search string produced a few results from Google (Figure 1.51). It is best to avoid using long quotations in searches, since any minor variations in the wording can result in no matches being obtained. In this case the name of the composer and part of the quotation was sufficient to produce some useful matches.

1 Web searching

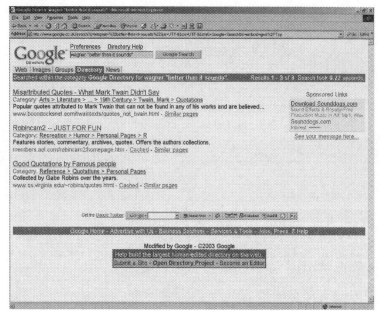

Fig.1.51 Google has found some results

Apparently Mark Twain did say these words, but he was quoting Bill Nye (Figure 1.52). There are actually sites that help find quotations, but in general it is better to use an ordinary search engine.

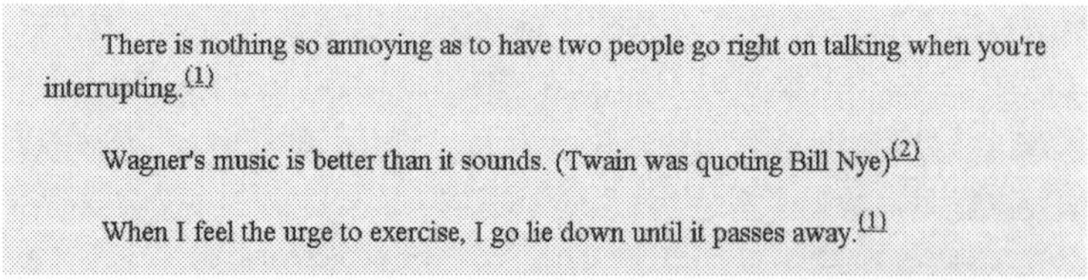

There is nothing so annoying as to have two people go right on talking when you're interrupting.[1]

Wagner's music is better than it sounds. (Twain was quoting Bill Nye)[2]

When I feel the urge to exercise, I go lie down until it passes away.[1]

Fig.1.52 One of the pages has the required answer

Points to remember

There are a number of good search engines, but Google has established itself as the market leader. Either Google or a Google-based search engine should be your first port of call when searching the Internet.

The usual problem these days is boiling the search results down to manageable proportions rather than finding any matches. Try to use a number of words in the search string in order to focus the search as tightly as possible. Using one or two words and then wading through thousands of matches is not the way to obtain quick results.

Google will automatically search for pages that contain all the search words. The more words you use, the fewer the matches that will be obtained. Placing a phrase in double quotes is a powerful weapon in getting the number of matches down to a reasonable figure. You need good quality results and not a large quantity of them.

If you are directed to a page that is not quite what you are looking for, take a quick look around the site to see if there is anything more useful. There might also be links to other sites containing useful information. Some search engines have a facility to look for sites that are similar to sites found in the initial search. Using this facility might produce a list containing a number of useful sites.

Where a complete blank is drawn, check that you are spelling all the search words correctly. Be especially careful when using phrases in double quotation marks. The web covers a vast range of subjects, but there are inevitably some subjects where there is little or no worthwhile information.

It would be a mistake to regard some of the more modern search engines as gimmicky. They are especially useful for those who find it difficult to master conventional search procedures. Even experienced users might find some types of search easier and quicker using a site such as AskJeeves.co.uk.

If the link to a page fails, operate the refresh button once or twice to make sure it is genuinely unavailable. Trying again later sometimes brings results. Where a page has been changed or deleted you may be able to glean some useful information from a cached version of the page, if it is available.

In cases where the exact page you require has definitely been deleted, the site that contained the page may still contain some useful information or links to other sites that have the information you require.

2

Specialist searches

Right approach

Going to a general search engine and typing in a few likely search words is not always the best way of going about things. There are specialist sites that deal with popular types of searches, and special facilities at some of the main search engines that deal with this type of thing. One obvious subject of this type is software. There are numerous sites that deal specifically with software downloads, such as Download.com. There are even sites that deal specifically with searching for software drivers. If you lose the installation disc for a piece of hardware in your PC, or perhaps a peripheral device such as a printer, these sites will help you locate the missing software on the Internet.

When you require a software download it makes sense to try one of the specialist sites first. You will probably find what you are after fairly rapidly, but you can always try a general search if the software sites do not locate something suitable. The same doctrine applies to several types of search, and a number of specialised searches are covered in this chapter.

Fig.2.1 Google has five modes of operation

Right image

A search engine should find information about any reasonably well known place or a person. If you are looking for a picture rather than information you might be lucky and "strike gold" right away, or you could end up wading through dozens of web pages. The chances of success are quite high with something like a famous place or person. In the previous chapter the search for the statue of Christ near Rio de Janeiro produced several photographs of the statue in amongst the historical and geographical information. With something less famous you would be more likely to find yourself going through dozens of pages before you found a suitable photograph.

The number of images available on the Web must be pretty staggering, and you will normally be able to find something suitable when a picture of a person, place, plant, or an animal is required. In fact there

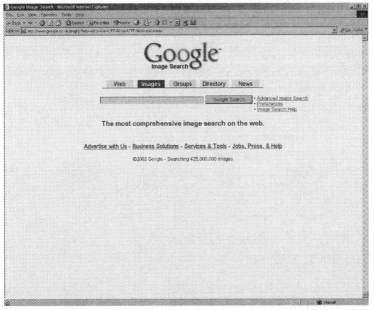

Fig.2.2 Things look much the same in Image mode

are pictures of all sorts of things on the Internet from household items to pictures of deep space. There are online picture agencies, specialist sites for tracking down images and image search facilities at some of the large search engines. The image searching facility of an ordinary search engine is probably the best option if you are not intending to buy images.

Figure 2.1 shows the upper part of the Google.co.uk homepage, and you will notice that there are five rectangular buttons above the textbox for the search string. The Web button is active by default, and the search engine therefore does a normal search of the Internet unless you tell it to do otherwise. We wish to

Fig.2.3 The search results include "thumbnails"

search for images, so the Images button is operated. The page will reload, but there is little change in its appearance (Figure 2.2). In fact the only conspicuous difference is that the Images button rather than the Web button is highlighted. Despite the lack of any major change in outward appearance, the search engine operates very differently in the Image search mode.

Using the search words "Rio", "Christ", and "statue" produced the page of results shown in Figure 2.3. This page contains numerous links to photographs of the correct place, and the additional pages of results contain many more. There is a small "thumbnail"

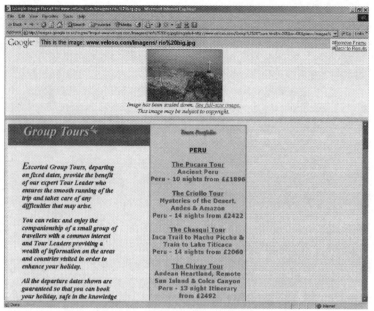

Fig.2.4 The page is split into two sections

version of each image above its link-text. Operating one of the links or left-clicking an image results in the page being split into two sections (Figure 2.4). A larger thumbnail version of the image is displayed in the upper section, and the page it came from is shown in the lower one.

Operating the "See full-size image" link near the bottom right-hand corner of the image results in it being displayed at its normal size in its own page (Figure 2.5). In general, web images are quite small, so the full-size version might not be much different to the small "thumbnail" image. In fact it might not be any bigger at all. Another way of viewing the image

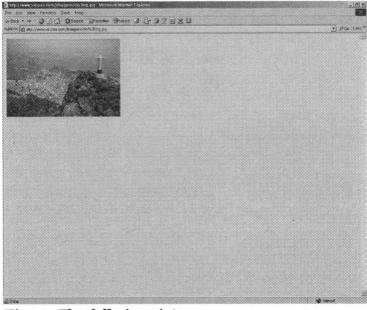

Fig.2.5 The full-size picture

full-size is to scroll down the web page in the lower
section of the screen until the image appears, as in
Figure 2.6.   There will often be some useful
information on the web page, so it is a good idea to at
least quickly look through it.

Focussed images

The image search facility will not produce results that
are one hundred percent relevant to your search, and
there will usually be a few images listed that seem to
have nothing to do with your search terms. In general
though, image searching facilities seem to provide
more focussed results than normal web searches.

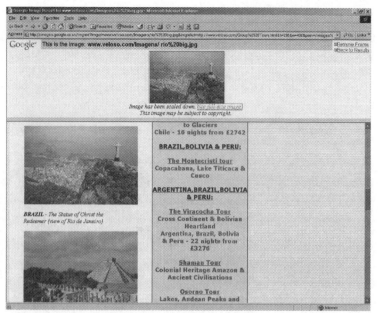

Fig.2.6 The picture is available in the lower frame

The small thumbnail images make it easy to spot the ones that are of no interest.

The statue used for this example is world famous, but image searches will usually produce a few useful results from places of lesser note. A search for "Southend" and "pier" produced numerous pictures, ancient and modern, of the world's longest pleasure pier. One example is shown in Figure 2.7. A search for "Wigan" and "pier" produced numerous links to the world's shortest pier, as made famous by George Orwell. One example is shown in Figure 2.8. Searching for "Neasden", "High", and "Street" failed to produce any results, but there were matches for

2 Specialist searches

Fig.2.7 A picture of Southend's pier

Fig.2.8 Wigan's pier proved to be no problem either

Fig.2.9 A picture of the temple, not the high street

Neasden, including the magnificent new temple (Figure 2.9).

People and animals

It is not only photographs of places that are available on the Internet, and there are plenty of pictures of famous people for example. Queen Victoria died over 100 tears ago, but a search based on her name produced an amazing 6270 results (Figure 2.10). Some of the links were to photographs of buildings named after her, statues of her, or documents she had signed. Most seemed to be portraits of Queen Victoria, and there was a mixture of paintings and photographs.

2 Specialist searches

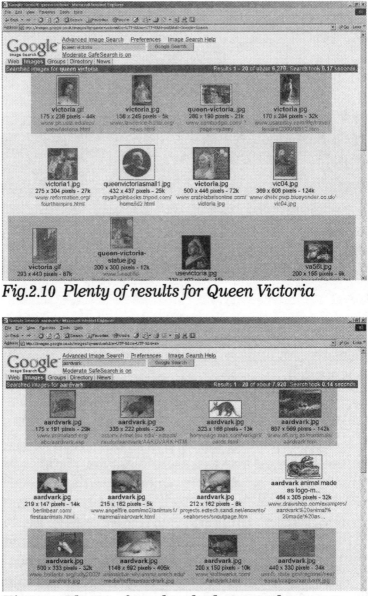

Fig.2.10 Plenty of results for Queen Victoria

Fig.2.11 Plenty of aardvark photographs

Fig.2.12 One of 46500 results for "zebra"

Surprisingly perhaps, pictures of pubs were not much in evidence.

Animals feature very prominently, and there seems to be pictures of just about everything from aardvarks (Figure 2.11) to zebras (Figure 2.12). Use the name of the animal as the search string, and unless it is something extremely rare you will be rewarded with links to at least a few photographs. In most cases there seems to be hundreds or even thousands of links. There was an astonishing 46500 links to zebra related photographs for instance. The highest number of matches I could get for a person was 8900 for John Wayne!

2 Specialist searches

Fig.2.13 There are photographs of collectables

You can often get quite good results from general searches. Suppose you are interested in collecting carnival glass. Using this as the search string produced links to pictures of more than 2000 items of carnival glass (Figure 2.13). Some of the photographs are literally out of this world. A search for pictures of the planet Mars produced not only long range views, but the famous picture of the Mars Rover vehicle exploring the rocky surface of the planet (Figure 2.14). Using "Neptune" as the search string produced links to numerous pictures of the other blue planet including pictures taken by the Hubble Space Telescope and the Voyager 2 probe (Figure 2.15). If

Fig.2.14 The Mars Rover in action

you are interested in astronomy you will be pleasantly surprised at the huge number of space related images on the Internet.

Unless you are after something pretty outlandish there should be no difficulty in tracking down an image of it on the Internet. If you have become used to struggling with ordinary web searches you will probably find searching for images remarkably easy. I find myself wondering "where's the catch", but for the most part it really is that straightforward.

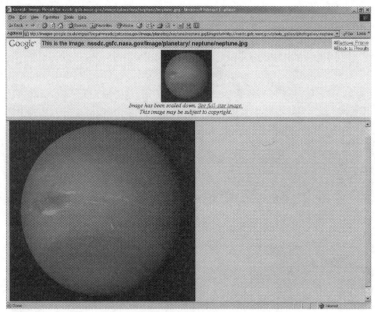

Fig.2.15 The other blue planet (Neptune)

Copyright

If you would like to save an image to disc or print it out there is usually no difficulty in doing so. However, there are copyright matters to bear in mind. Many of the images on the Internet are in the public domain, which simply means that no one owns the copyright on them. With an old image this can be due to the copyright having lapsed. With more recent images it can be the result of the original owner of the image allowing the copyright to lapse. In other words, they have decided to place the image in the public domain and relinquish their copyright.

A substantial proportion of the pictures on the Internet are the subject of copyright, and there will either be a copyright notice on each image or one governing the site as a whole. The situation is complicated by the fact that many people illegally use copyright material on their web sites. Although there is no copyright notice on their site, the images are actually the property of someone else and are in copyright. Using images from the Internet in any way that could be a breach of copyright is therefore a bit risky.

Simply looking at images on the Internet is not a breach of copyright. Downloading them onto your PC so they can be viewed later or making prints of them certainly could be a breach of copyright. Being realistic about things though, it is unlikely that anyone is going to be too bothered about this sort of personal use. Videoing television programs so that you can view them later is not strictly legal either, but the owners of the copyright do not get "hot under the collar" about this sort of time-shifting.

Sending images to friends of relatives in either electronic or printed form is more dubious, and is best avoided unless you are sure that doing so will not infringe anyone's copyright. Any sort of commercial use, such as downloading images and then selling them as picture postcards or framed images, would certainly be an infringement of copyright. For this type of thing you need to be sure that the images are in the public domain, and you must get permission to use them if they are subject to copyright. Using copyright material is almost certain to involve the payment of a fee.

Saving images

Saving images to disc is very straightforward, but it is slightly different depending on the browser you use. Assuming that you are using a reasonably modern version of Internet Explorer, placing the pointer over an image will result in a bar with four icons appearing near what is usually the top left-hand corner of the image (Figure 2.16). This is a small toolbar, and each icon is actually a button. The leftmost button has an icon that depicts a 3.5-inch floppy disc, and this one is left-clicked if you wish to save the image. A file browser then appears (Figure 2.17), and this is used to save the file in standard Windows fashion.

Fig.2.16 The toolbar

The default name of the image might be something descriptive, but it will often just be a serial number or something of this type. In order to change the name, first drag the cursor through the text in the File name field to select it. In other words, move the

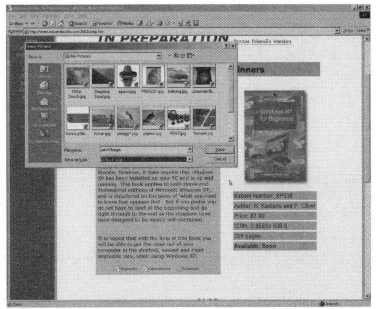

Fig.2.17 The usual Windows file browser appears

cursor through the text while holding down the left mouse button. The text and its background will change colour to indicate that it has been sleeted. Then simply type in the new name which will replace the old one.

The Save as type menu enables the image to be saved in a different file format, but the options available here will be strictly limited. The vast majority of images on the Internet are in either the Jpeg (also called Jpg) or GIF formats. These are compatible with virtually all programs that can handle graphics files, so there will usually be no point in changing to a different type. The Save in field near the top of the window enables

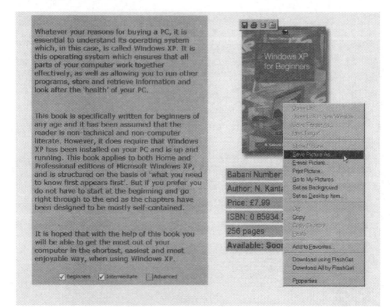

Fig.2.18 The popup menu offers print facilities

the file to be saved in a location other than the default one, which is usually the Pictures folder. This is a subfolder of the My Documents folder. It is probably worthwhile making a separate folder for web images if you will be saving a lot of them to disc. When everything is set correctly, operate the Save button to go ahead and save the file to disc.

An alternative way of going about things is to right-click on the image, which will produce a popup menu like the one shown in Figure 2.18. The Save Picture file browser is launched by selecting the Save Picture As option. Things then proceed in the manner described previously. Note that this will be the only

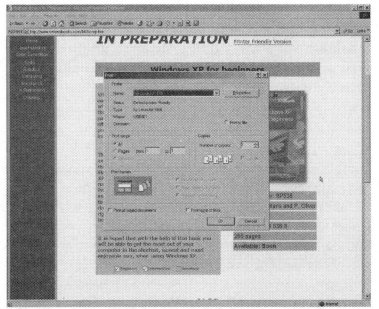

Fig.2.19 The Print window is printer-specific

way of saving images if you are using an old version of Internet Explorer. It will also be the only way of saving an image if it is acting as a link.

Printing

If your PC is equipped with a printer it is possible to print Internet images. With a modern version of Internet Explorer, start by placing the pointer over the image to make the small toolbar appear. Then left-click the second button from the left, which is the one that has an icon depicting a printer. This brings up the Print dialogue box (Figure 2.19), but note that this is different for each printer. Usually there are options to change things like the orientation of the picture and the print quality, but the exact facilities available vary from one printer to another. The instruction manual for your printer should give a detailed explanation of the available options.

When any necessary adjustments have been made, operate the OK button to go ahead and print the image. This way of doing things is delightfully simple, but it has a major drawback in that you do not usually have any control over the size of the printed image. Printing via an image editing program such as Photoshop Elements gives much more versatility. You can, for example, choose the size of the print if you download the image, load it into an image editing program, and print it from there. Most images will print at quite small sizes by default, but it is not practical to print most web images at large sizes anyway. Web images are built up from thousands of dots of different colours, or "pixels" as they are called. A typical web image would have something like 300 rows of pixels with about 400 pixels in each row. This gives 120,000 pixels in the image, which sounds quite impressive.

Unfortunately, a full size image on an ordinary A4 size inkjet printer requires about three million pixels in order to produce high quality results. For good quality results it is necessary to have not much less than 200 pixels to the inch, or about 80 pixels to the centimetre if you are into metrication. Printing at anything much less than this will result in the individual dots being discernible instead of merging into a "seamless" image. Trying to print a 400 by 300 pixel image at much more than about 2 inches by 1.5 inches will therefore give rather poor print quality. Of course, some web images are much bigger than 400 by 300 pixels, but even at 800 by 600

Fig.2.20 Netscape's popup menu

pixels the maximum print size should be kept to not much more than about 4 inches by 3 inches.

Netscape

Saving and printing images is handled in a similar fashion if you are using a browser other than Internet Explorer. Netscape Navigator lacks the popup toolbar, but right-clicking on an image produces a menu (Figure 2.20) that includes a Save Image As option. Selecting this produces the Save Picture file browser, and the file is then saved to disc in the usual way. As far as I am aware, Navigator does not have a facility for directly printing images, only complete pages. It does have a facility for setting the selected image as wallpaper, and there is a facility in Internet

Explorer for setting the image as the background. These have the same function, which is to use the image as the background for the Windows desktop.

You will sometimes find that the usual methods of saving a picture to disc do not work. This is not usually due to a fault in the software or the web site, and is done deliberately by the site's creator in an attempt to prevent the images from being downloaded. This is used as a means of protecting the copyright in the images. There are probably ways around protection measures, but if the owners of a site do not wish you to download the images to disc it is only fair to respect their wishes. Copying the images would almost certainly be illegal.

Music

A huge amount of music is available on the Internet, but as one would expect, a high percentage of this is modern pop music. This is good news if you are into the latest mega-funk-rock-grunge, or whatever. The amount on offer is rather less if you are primarily interested in classical music, easy listening, or jazz. There is actually quite a lot of "golden oldie" pop music for those who like to get nostalgic about the 1960s and 1970s.

Music on the web breaks down into two broad categories, which is the type that you download to disc and then play using a suitable program, and streaming audio. A suitable media player program is needed in order to play music that is saved to disc, but most music files can be played using the Windows Media Player that is normally installed as part of Windows. It is also available as a free download from the Microsoft web site (www.microsoft.com).

Streaming audio is normally played more or less as it is received. Because the stream of data often tends to be a bit intermittent it is normal for a certain amount of the audio data to be stored in the computer's memory before the player program starts to play it. This store of data is called a "buffer". The general idea is that the buffer will ensure that the player program does not run out of data during any gaps in the stream from the server. Of course, the buffer will run out of data if the data stream is interrupted too often or for too long. Unfortunately, this does sometimes occur, particularly when using streaming audio over an ordinary dialup connection.

A broadband connection is definitely an advantage in any application that involves downloading large amounts of data, which includes streaming audio. There is no guarantee that an adequate flow of data will be maintained even when using the broadest of broadband Internet connections. There can be problems somewhere in the system, or the server providing the data can simply become overloaded. Gaps in streaming audio just have to be accepted as one of the "joys" of modern computing.

Some streaming audio can be handled by the Windows Media Player, but it is often necessary to use either a special player or the Real OnePlayer program. A web site that provides any form of audio file or streaming audio should include details of the player program required, and where it can be downloaded. This type of program is usually free, but there might be the option of buying a "deluxe" version. Where appropriate, the player program must be installed before you can start listening to the audio.

Formats

Ideally there would be just one format for audio on the Internet, but this is the world of computing, and things are simply not done that way. It is traditional to have at least two competing technologies, and preferably about half a dozen. The nearest thing to a standard audio format is MP3, which is the format used by those little Walkman style audio players that are so popular with the younger generation. The Windows Media Player program will play MP3 files, as will most player programs.

When dealing with MP3 you will encounter references to "bit rates". The higher the bit rate, the higher the technical quality of the audio signal. A rate of about 128 kilobits (128,000 bits) per second or more is needed for high quality stereo listening. A rate of 96 kilobits per second is all right, but anything lower can start to sound "a bit rough at the edges".

WMA (Windows media audio) is the main rival to MP3. Many feel that it is technically superior to MP3, but it has never achieved the same degree of support. That is not to say that it is little used, and there are vast numbers of WMA files available on the Internet. MP3 and WMA files are mainly used on the basis of a file being downloaded and then played once the complete file has been stored on your PC. They can be used for a form of streaming audio as well, but only if your Internet connection and the rest of the system can handle the relatively high data rates involved. Unless you have some form of broadband connection such as an ADSL or cable type, it is unlikely that these will be usable in streaming form.

The more usual choice for streaming audio is the Real Audio (RA) format, and as mentioned previously, this requires the special player program that is free in its most basic form. While Real Audio permits streaming even with an ordinary 56k dialup connection, the low flow of data inevitably imposes some restrictions on the audio quality. There can be some odd background noises when using Real Audio with a slow connection, but the same is true of any other system when it is used with a low bit rate. Whether or not the audio quality is worthwhile is a subjective matter. Probably most people will be happy with the low audio quality for something like the news or a sports commentary, but not for most types of music.

Video

These days it is possible to download videos on the Internet, but there are practical problems. Streamed audio has to be something less than hi-fi when used with an ordinary dialup Internet connection, and even more compromises have to be made with video. The picture quality is poor and very jerky, and the sound quality leaves a lot to be desired. On the face of it, these problems can be overcome by downloading the movie and then playing it back. This is fine, but only for short video clips. With audio and video the amounts of data can be quite large.

An audio CD usually contains about 500 to 700 megabytes of data. By using an audio format such as MP3 or WMA this can be reduced to about 30 to 50 megabytes without seriously compromising the technical quality. Using an ADSL broadband connection it is possible to download just over three megabytes of data in a minute, so it is actually possible to download an audio file in less time than it takes to play it. The same is not true of video, but it is still possible to download video of moderate quality in about the same time as it takes to play. It follows from this that it is possible to have reasonably good quality streaming video with a broadband connection.

With a 56k dialup connection the download rate is about one megabyte every three or four minutes rather than three or four megabytes per one minute. To download an hour of music would therefore take at least a couple or hours or so. Not exactly quick, but still well within reason. In order to download an hour of reasonable quality video using a real world 56k connection would take more like 10 to 20 hours. While this is not totally out of the question, probably few users would deem it worth the effort.

There is a video version of Real Audio, and this format is often used for streamed video. It can be handled by the free Real One Player program. Some sites use WMV (Windows media video), which can be played using the Windows Media Player. There are two main formats that are used for downloading video files, and these are Mpeg (or Mpg) and AVI. Mpeg can be played using the Windows Media Player, and most other media player programs that can handle video. The quality is usually quite good, but the file sizes are relatively large.

Codecs

AVI has become increasingly popular, and it can provide smaller file sizes than an equivalent Mpeg movie. However, to my eyes at least, the quality is not as good as that provided by an Mpeg movie. In the quest for ever smaller file sizes it is now quite common for AVI files to have additional processing. They can still be played back by the Windows Media Player, but only if it is equipped with some additional software. This software is called a codec, or coder/ decoder. It is actually only the decoder that is needed, but it is still termed a codec even though it only decodes.

The most common codec is the DivX type, but this exists in several versions. Provided your PC is equipped with the latest one, it should be able to deal with any version of DivX. The site offering the download should make it clear what codec, if any, is needed in order to play the movie. It should also provide details of where to obtain the codec and obtain

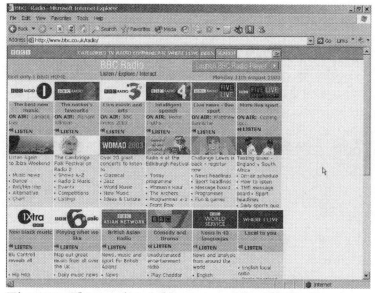

Fig.2.21 The main radio page of the BBC site

installation details. The Windows Media Player will sometimes detect that a codec is needed, and then look for it on the web if there is an active Internet connection. It might locate and successfully install the codec, but the automatic method does not seem to be totally reliable. The manual method seems to give a much better chance of success.

You may well encounter video and audio formats other than those mentioned here. Again, the site providing the download or streamed material should give details of any special players or codecs that are needed. Make sure that you have or can obtain any necessary player software or codec prior to starting a long download.

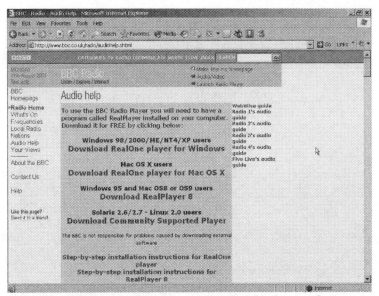

Fig.2.22 The Help screen provides links to the download site

Radio

Internet radio stations are stations that provide their programs on the Internet via streamed audio. In most cases they also transmit their programs via radio signals, but in some cases they only use the Internet. As one would probably expect, in the UK the BBC is the largest provider of Internet radio. The place to start is www.bbc.co.uk/radio (Figure 2.21). All the main BBC stations are now available via the Internet, including the digital stations such as Radio 7. In general, the BBC local radio stations are not available via this route, but their sports commentaries are often made available on the Internet.

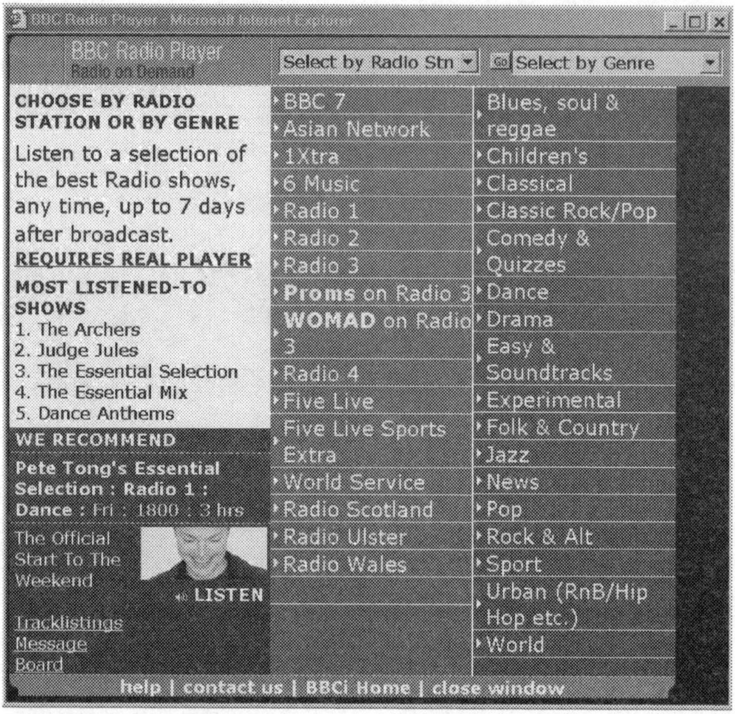

Fig.2.23 The BBC version of the Real Player

In order to listen to the BBC stations it is necessary to have the Real One Player installed on your PC. If it is not already installed, operating one of the Help links will produce the page shown in Figure 2.22. This gives links to download sites for the player, together with other useful information about installing and using it. Once installed, the player can be started by left-clicking the Launch BBC Radio Player link on the radio homepage. Figure 2.23 shows the player after launch, and it does not look anything like the normal version of the Real One Player.

Fig.2.24 The BBC player program in operation

This player, like most of the others, has the ability to use shells. A shell changes the appearance of the player program, and possibly its functionality as well, but it is still basically the standard player. In the case of the BBC version the central column enables the required station to be selected, as does the drop-down menu at the top of the column. Note that due to the use of buffering by media players the Internet version of a station can lag its normal radio counterpart by several seconds, or even longer if a large buffer is used. This is built into the system, so it occurs with all Internet radio stations and not just those of the BBC. If you are going to use the time pips to set your watch, tune into the BBC using a radio rather than using the Internet.

The text to either side of the central column mainly provides links to recorded material such as the latest episode of the Archers and popular comedy programs

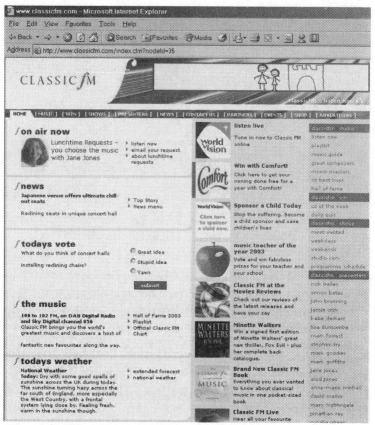

Fig.2.25 The Classic FM homepage

and quizzes. Recorded programs, like the "live" variety, are in the form of streamed audio. Figure 2.24 shows the player in operation, and the usual tape recorder style controls have appeared in the left-hand section of the window. The facilities on offer here depend on whether the program is "live" or recoded.

Although the audio quality is not bad, it is something less than true hi-fi. It is remarkably good considering the slow bit-rate used, which does not require a broadband connection. With the FM stations you are probably better off listening via any semi-decent radio, but the Internet often provides better quality audio than you would get from an AM station. The main advantage from the Internet for many users is that is provides access to the digital stations. If you are using some form of non-metered Internet access you get these stations more or less free of charge. Any streamed audio or video could be quite expensive for those using some form of metered Internet access.

Commercial radio

The BBC is not the only source of UK radio stations on the Internet. Classic FM is available from their web site at:

www.classicfm.com

Figure 2.25 shows the Classic FM homepage, and the link to the online version of the station is in the On Air Now section near the top left-hand corner of the page. Left-click the Listen Now link and then do the same again on the link in the top left-hand corner of the next page that appears (Figure 2.26).

Fig.2.26 *Operate the Listen Now Link*

Fig.2.27 The Classic FM player in operation

The radio player will then be launched (Figure 2.27) and you can listen to the station. At one time it was necessary to download a small program called an "applet" in order to listen to Classic FM online, but these days it seems to utilize the Windows Media Player.

Fig.2.28 The Jazz FM homepage

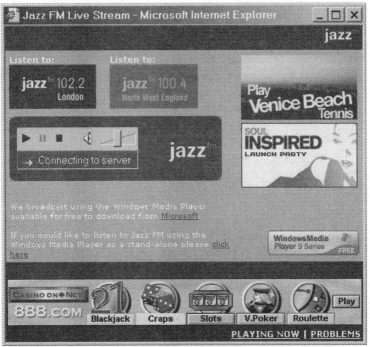

Fig.2.29 The Jazz FM player in operation

Like Classic FM, Jazz FM is where you would expect to find it on the Internet, which is at:

www.jazzfm.com

The homepage is shown in Figure 2.28. In order to listen to this station just activate the Listen to Jazz FM link, which will launch the player (Figure 2.29).

The UK stations of Virgin Radio are also available online from their UK homepage at:

www.virginradio.co.uk

Figure 2.30 shows the homepage, and the Listen Now

Fig.2.30 The Virgin Radio homepage

menu is used to access the online station. Placing
the pointer over the menu heading produces the pop-
down menu, and Listen Now is then selected from
the menu. This produces the page of Figure 2.31
where the required station is selected by left-clicking
its link. In Figure 2.32 the Virgin Radio Classic Rock
station has been selected and is happily playing away.
Note that you might have to download and install an
applet in order to listen to the stations in stereo.
However, all you have to do is operate the appropriate

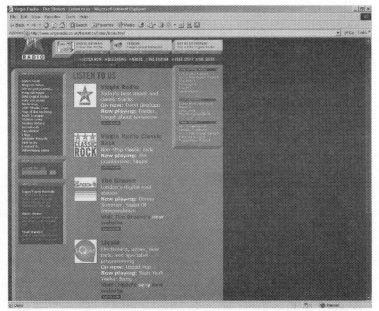

Fig.2.31 Select the required station using its link

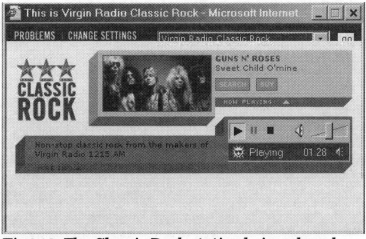

Fig.2.32 The Classic Rock station being played

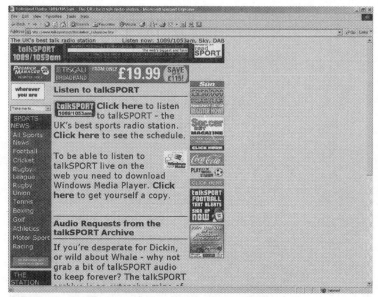

Fig.2.33 Talk Sport is also on the Internet

button when prompted. Installation is then fully automatic.

Talk Sport Radio is also available online, and their web site is at:

http://www.talksport.net

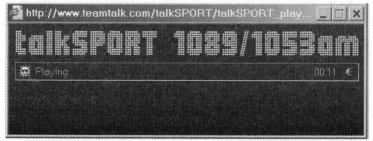

Fig.2.34 The player for Talk Sport Radio

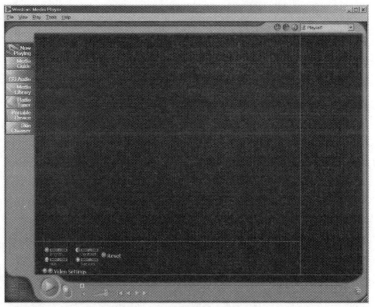

Fig.2.35 The Windows Media Player

There is a Listen Now link in the large column of links down the left side of the homepage, but you will probably have to scroll down the page to reveal it. Activating this link produces the page of Figure 2.33, and left-clicking the appropriate link launches the player program (Figure 2.34).

Radio Tuner

There are many more radio stations available on the Internet, and it is not difficult to track them down using an ordinary search engine such as Google. An alternative approach is to use the Radio Tuner function of the Windows Media Player. Either launch

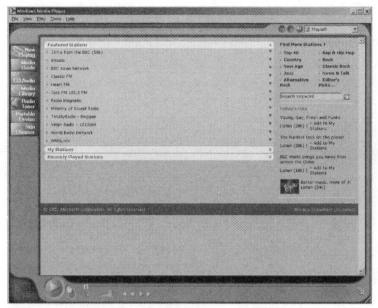

Fig.2.36 Using the Radio Tuner facility

the player by double-clicking its icon on the desktop, or go to the Run menu, select programs, and then search for its entry in the list. Left-click the player's entry to launch the program. The appearance of the player will depend on the version you are using and its operating mode. Figure 2.35 shows version seven

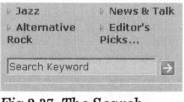

Fig.2.37 The Search textbox

running in Full mode. If the player is running in Compact mode it will be necessary to operate the button in the bottom right-hand corner in order to place it in Full mode.

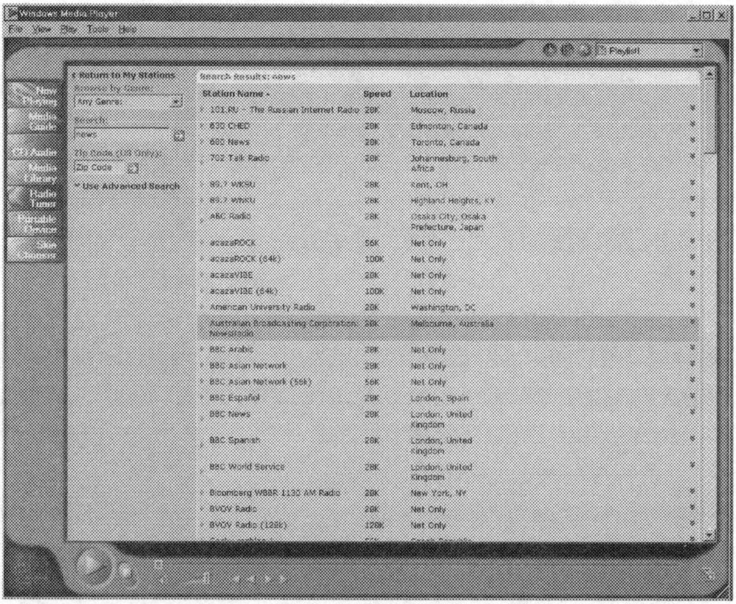

Fig.2.38 The search results for "news"

To use the Radio Tuner facility it is merely necessary to operate the button of this name on the left side of the window. The player will then look something like Figure 2.36. The left section of the main panel shows various stations that are available, and a number of categories are available in the right-hand section. There is also a search facility in this section, so you can type a search string into the textbox (Figure 2.37) and then operate the button with the arrow icon to proceed with the search. Figure 2.38 shows the result of using "news" as the search string.

In order to play a station it is merely necessary to operate the tiny green triangular button next to its

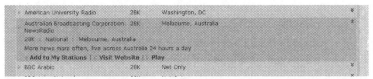

Fig.2.39 Left-click an entry to show its options

entry. Alternatively, left-clicking the entry itself will produce two or three options (Figure 2.39), and these will usually include the options of playing the station or visiting the corresponding web site. The entry for each station includes a bit rate, such as "28k". Most stations can be used with an ordinary 56k Internet

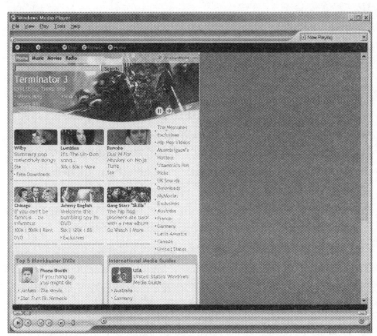

Fig.2.40 Version 9 of the Windows Media Player

connection, but for anything higher than this some sort of broadband connection is required.

If you are using Windows Media Player 9 it is possible that the taskbar will not be present down the left-hand side of the window (Figure 2.40). However, there will be a narrow button having an arrow icon about halfway up the left-hand side of the

Fig.2.41 The thin button

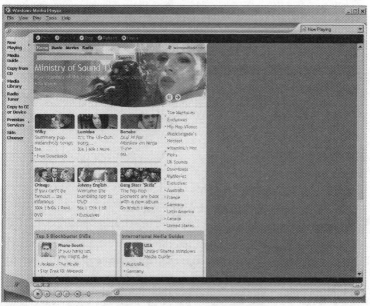

Fig.2.42 The taskbar is now displayed

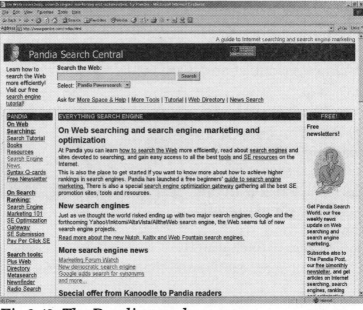

Fig.2.43 The Pandia.com homepage

window (Figure 2.41), and operating this button will result in the taskbar miraculously appearing (Figure 2.42). The player can then be used to search for radio stations in much the same way as its predecessors.

Radio search

As pointed out previously, you can seek out Internet radio stations using an ordinary search engine, and the searches are likely to be quite successful. However, there are special search engines for this type of thing as well as specialist search facilities at some general search sites. A useful general site with an Internet radio search facility can be found at:

www.pandia.com

Figure 2.43 shows the home page, and the important thing here is the Select menu near the top of the page.

This enables various types of search to be carried out, including one for Internet radio stations (Figure 2.44). Figure 2.45 shows the

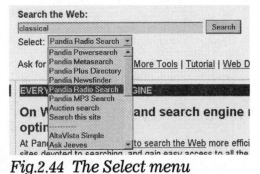

Fig.2.44 The Select menu

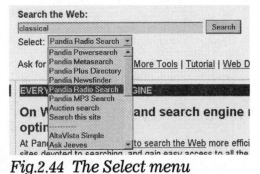

Fig.2.45 The search results for "classical"

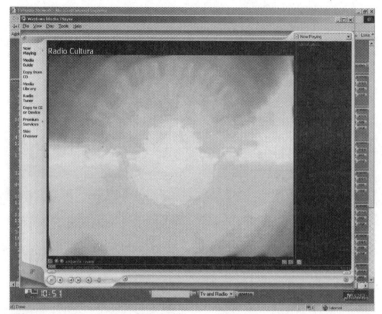

Fig.2.46 Here Radio Cultura is being played

result of using "classical" as the search string, and numerous stations from all over the world have matched this word.

The buttons in the right-hand section of the window show the available download rates for each station, and separate buttons are available for the Real One Player and the Windows Media Player. Only the buttons that have a green "light" are active, and operating one of these will launch the appropriate player and connect it to the seleted station. Figure 2.46 shows Radio Cultura being played, and this seems to be the Argentinean equivalent of Classic FM or BBC Radio 3.

*Fig.2.47 A list of stations can be produced for a
country or a state of the USA*

In addition to the search results, the Pandia search
engine provides a list of countries and states of the
USA down the left-hand side of the window. Left-
clicking on one of these countries or states produces
a list of the stations for that area (Figure 2.47). The
Category menu enables the results to be filtered to
stations of just one type (easy listening, folk, etc.).
This method has been used in Figure 2.48, which
shows the sports stations for Australia. Surprisingly
perhaps, there are only three of them!

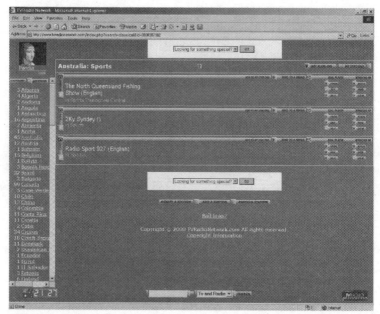

Fig.2.48 Just three sports stations for Australia!

Television

There are hundreds of Internet radio stations. In fact many stations that previously relied on shortwave transmitters to spread their programs around the world now use satellite, cable, and the Internet as their main means of distribution. Television is, of course, widely distributed using cable and satellite technology, but it has yet to make much impact on the Internet. The main problem is that it requires a broadband connection to produce anything approaching to normal broadcast quality. It also requires expensive hi-tech equipment to supply broadband television to a significant number of users.

If you go in search of
Internet television
stations it is likely that
you will find a large
number, but most of
them are not really true
equivalents of normal
television stations. Even
with Internet radio you
find that some of the
stations are actually
providing recorded

Fig.2.49 Operate the
appropriate link

programs and not a "live" stream of their normal
output. With Internet television this seems to be the

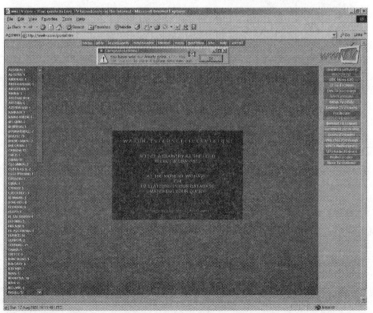

Fig.2.50 Choose from all or broadband stations

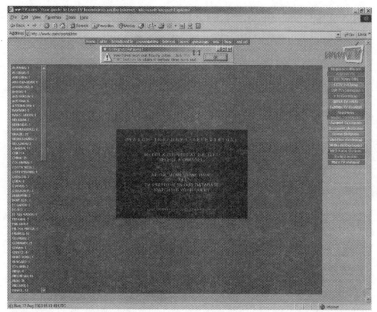

Fig.2.51 Left-click a country in the list on the left

norm, and many of the "live" stations are only available for a limited time each day.

The recorded stations can still be quite useful of course. The recorded news bulletins for example, are usually quite up to date. The advantage of this system is that you always start at the beginning of the program, whereas you have to connect at the right time in order to catch the beginnings of "live" programs. If you wish to go in search of Internet television stations, this is a good place to start:

www.wwitv.com

Start by left-clicking the "CLICK HERE to watch TV" link (Figure 2.49), and in the next page opt to watch

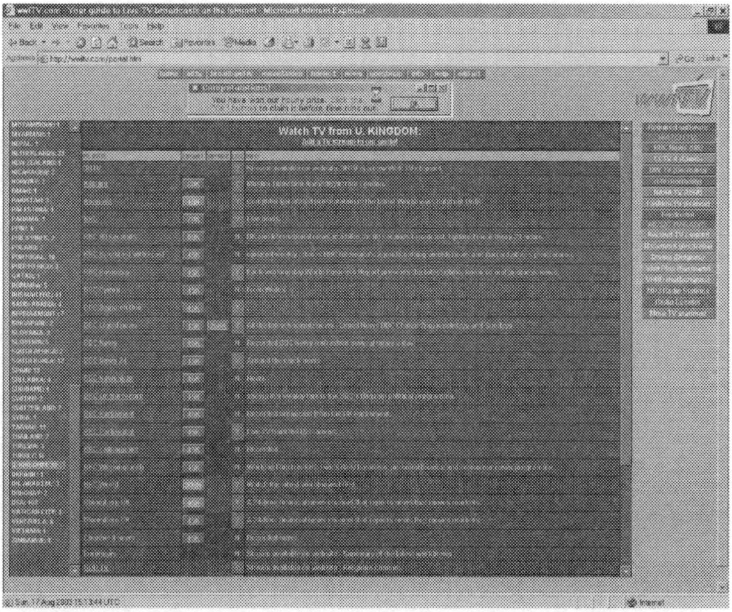

Fig.2.52 A list of stations for the selected country

either all stations or only the broadband variety (Figure 2.50). I opted for all stations, which produced the page of Figure 2.51. Left-clicking one of the countries listed down the left-hand side produces a list of stations from that country (Figure 2.52). Operating one of the buttons will launch the appropriate media player, which will play the station if it is available.

Figure 2.53 shows the UK version of Bloomberg TV being played in the Windows Media Player. This station is a good one for financial news and comment, and it is one of the few in the UK that is streamed "live" for 24 hours per day. The BBC News 24 station

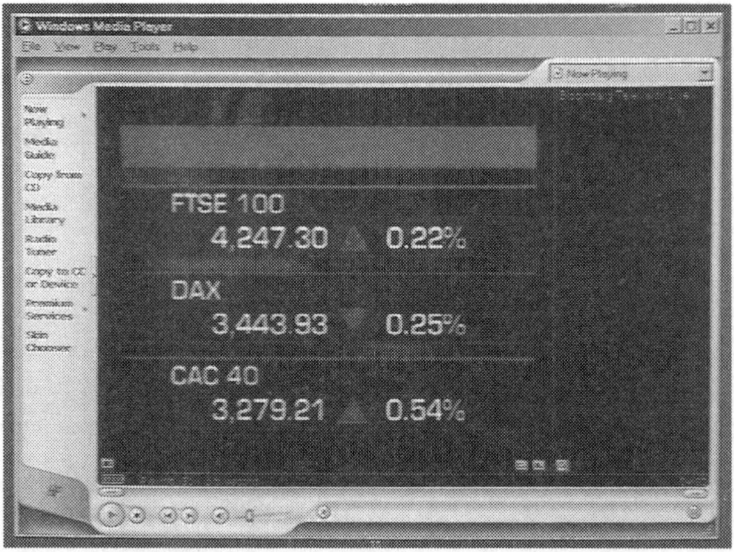

Fig.2.53 Financial news from Bloomberg TV

is another station that is online for 24 hours per day, but neither of these stations offers a broadband option. The video is therefore pretty crude. Stations from around the world are available, and Figure 2.54 shows a broadband Australian news station playing in the Real One Player. This is recorded and not a "live" feed though.

Internet television is still very much in its infancy. Connecting to some stations can be difficult, and will not necessarily be worth the effort involved. Some stations are only available if you go through a registration process, and a few can only be viewed if a fee is paid. It is interesting to view some of the free stations though, and there is a reasonable selection

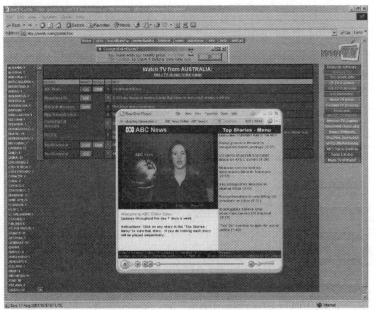

Fig.2.54 An Australian news station

on offer from around the world. Presumably more variety will be offered in the coming years and the technical quality will improve.

Finding music

There is clearly a lot of music available on the Internet via radio and television stations, but music and music videos are available from many other sources. It has to be pointed out right away that much of the music that is available for download on the Internet is "bootleg" or "pirate" material. In other words, it is stuff that people have copied from legitimate sources and made available in breach of copyright. It is almost

113

certainly illegal to download and listen to most of this material even if it is only for personal use. The high cost of pirated material to the music industry due to lost royalties has resulted in a more aggressive approach to dealing with those that upload and download this material. It is advisable to steer well clear of any music that might be illegal.

If you put something like "free MP3 jazz" into a search engine it is likely that many thousands of matches will be produced. Some of them will probably link to legitimate sites, but many will link to "pirate" sites. Many of these sites do not actually contain anything to download, but are instead designed to con users into activating links to other sites. This generates revenues for the owners of the con sites. Anything you can actually download from a pirate site has to be treated with suspicion, as it could well contain a virus, Trojan, or other "nasty" that could damage your files or compromise the security of your PC.

Of course, there is plenty of legitimate music available on the Internet, and some of it is free. The free music falls into two general categories. Some is top quality material from famous artists, but it is usually in the form of streamed audio or video rather than files that can be downloaded and played over and over again. The second type is from up and (they hope) coming bands or individuals who use the Internet as a means of advertising their talents. They provide the material for free as it is unlikely that many would be prepared to pay for music from unknowns.

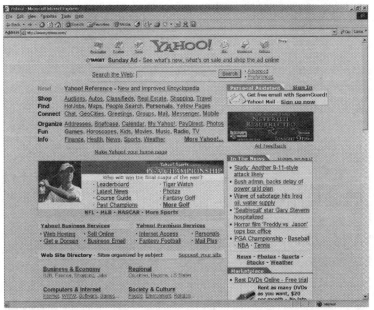

Fig.2.55 The Music link is in the Fun section

There seems to be an ever increasing number of sites that offer music on the basis of so much per download, or via a subscription that permits a certain number of downloads per month. This method of distribution should be very cheap, since the record companies do not have to press CDs, get sleeve notes prepared and printed, and so on. In general the subscriptions seem to offer good value for money if you wish to download large amounts of music. Some of the pay per track systems do not look particularly attractive, and could work out more expensive per track than buying a CD!

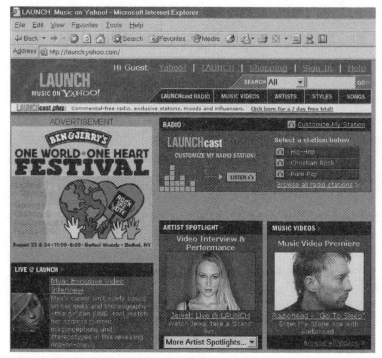

Fig.2.56 There is a search facility (top right)

Legitimate sites

Some free music is available from the Launch service of the Yahoo! site at:

www.yahoo.com

There is also a UK version at:

www.yahoo.co.uk

At either site, start by left-clicking the Music link in the Fun section (Figure 2.55). This produces a page like the one shown in Figure 2.56, and there is a search

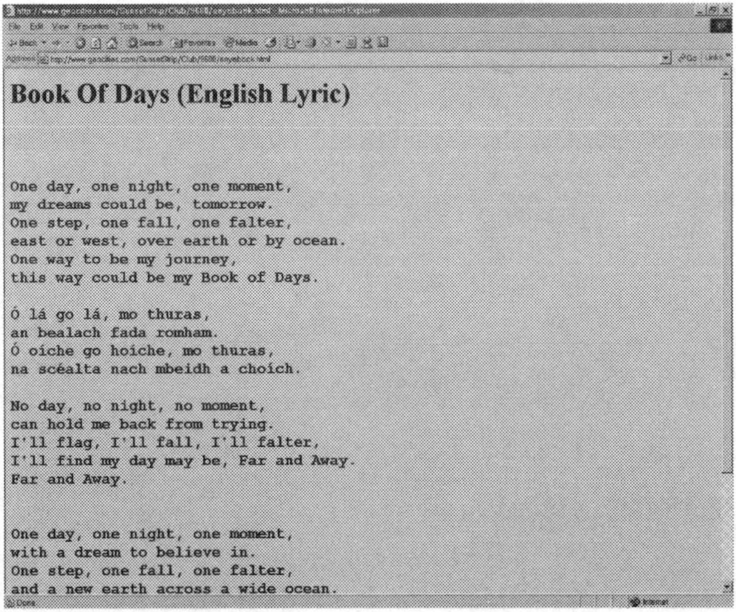

*Fig.2.57 Links to other sites provide reviews and
            (as here) lyrics*

facility near the top right-hand corner of the page. Try searches using the names of your favourite recording artists. A search for "Kate Bush" did not produce anything of great interest, but "Enya" was more fruitful. There were four videos listed, with some quite high bit-rates available for broadband users. Yahoo! has a wider range of music available on subscription, but only for those living in the USA or Canada. There are useful links to pages having reviews of the music, lyrics for the songs (Figure 2.57), news about the artist, etc. Yahoo!'s Launch service is well worth trying, but it only deals with music that is contemporary or from the recent past.

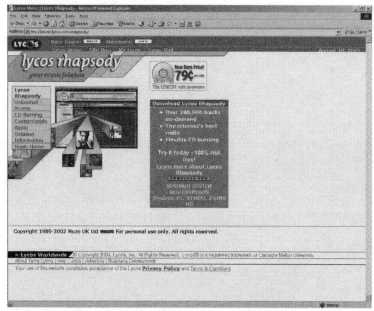

Fig.2.58 The Rhapsody facility at Lycos

Lycos has a similar facility to the subscription version of Launch, and this service is called Rhapsody (Figure 2.58). A limited trial of the service is available to anyone, but the main service is only available to those residing in North America. Possibly the Yahoo! and Lycos subscription services will be made more widely available in the future.

Classical music

A subscription service for classical music is available from:

www.classical.com

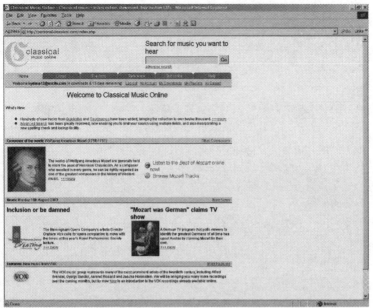

Fig.2.59 The Classical Music Online homepage

There is a free trial of their service, but it is only available to music libraries! However, a free 15 day trial is available from the personal version of the site (Classical Music Online) at:

http://personal.classical.com

Figure 2.59 shows the Classical Music Online homepage. You have to go through several forms during the signup process, and the first one is shown in Figure 2.60. It is not necessary to provide any credit card details, but it is a requirement that an Email address is provided. When obtaining freebies on the Internet it is usual for there to be a registration process first, and this will usually require you to supply an email address.

119

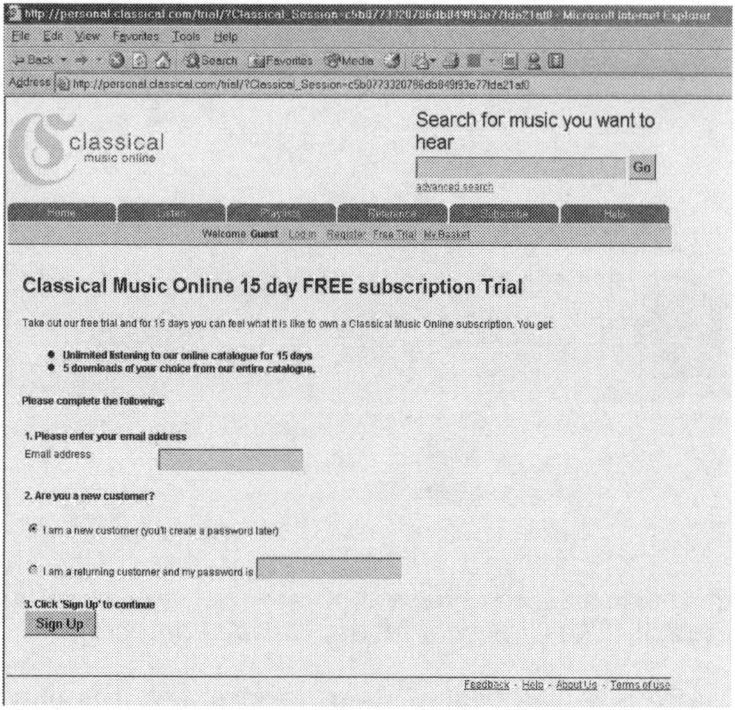

Fig.2.60 The first form in the registration process

Most companies will not pester you with numerous unsolicited Emails, but it is as well to play safe and open an Email account with one of the free online Email services such as Yahoo! or Microsoft's Hotmail. If anyone should start bombarding you with Emails, they will go to your dummy account and not to your main Email address. You should visit the dummy account from time to time in order to keep it active and delete any Emails that have accumulated, but it can otherwise be ignored.

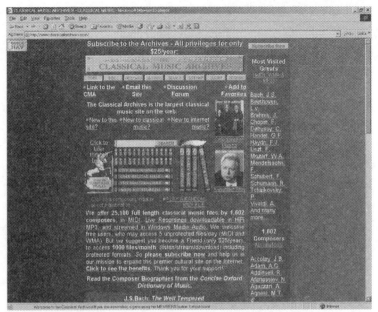

Fig.2.61 The Classical Music Archives site

The Classical Music Archives (Figure 2.61) claims to be the largest classical music site on the web, with over 25,000 full length classical music files. The homepage of this site is at:

http://www.classicalarchives.com/

It costs 25 US dollars (about 15 GB pounds at the time of writing) per year to subscribe to this site. A certain amount of free access is also available, but the streamed audio for non-paying users is at a relatively low rate. You have to pay the subscription in order to download files and obtain higher streaming rates. Unusually, it does not seem to be necessary to register with the site in order to access the free content. The

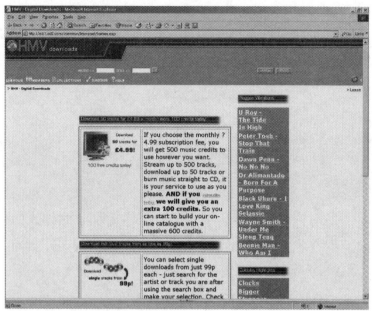

Fig.2.62 The download section of the HMV site

music on offer is mainly the older variety where the compositions have gone out of copyright, but I guess that many would consider this a blessing.

General

If you require a subscription site that has a massive amount to download, then this one is definitely worth a look:

www.hmv.co.uk

You can buy CDs, DVDs, etc., from this site, but somewhere on the homepage you should find a link to the download section (Figure 2.62). Here you can

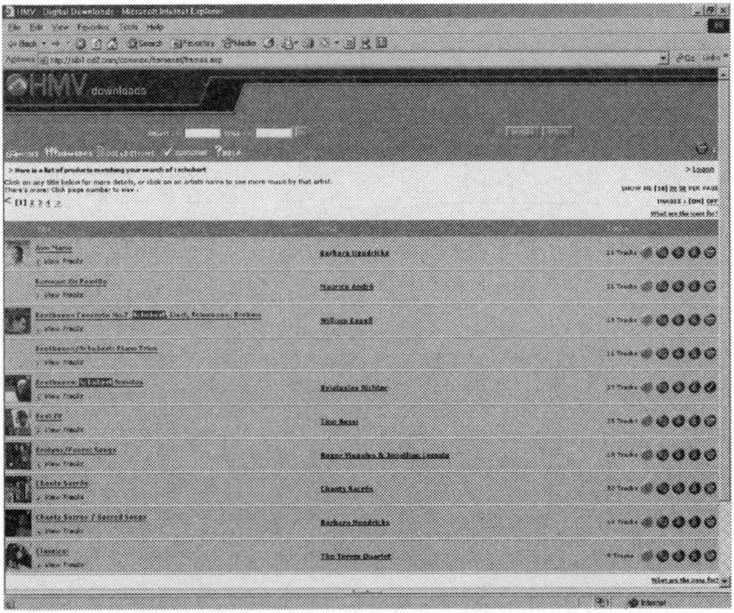

Fig.2.63 The search results for "Schubert"

search for music by artist or title, and Figure 2.63
shows the result of using "Schubert" in the Title field.
The buttons down the right-hand side of the page
provide various options. These are streaming the
entire CD, downloading it to your PC, burning a CD
using your PC, and buying the normal CD. Of course,
you need a PC equipped with a CD writer in order to
burn your own CDs, although most modern PCs are
suitably equipped for this task. Left-clicking on an
entry for a CD produces a list of its tracks (Figure
2.64). A free 30-second sample of each track is
available, and there are options to stream, download,
or burn each track.

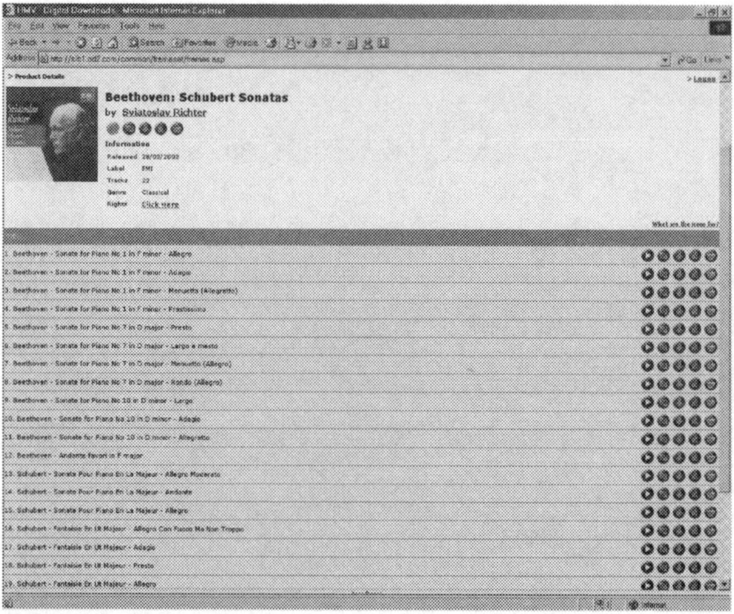

Fig.2.64 A list of tracks can be produced

The cost of burning CDs seems to be comparable to buying the "real thing", and at about one pound per individual track this does not seem to be a worthwhile option either. Streaming and downloading are paid for using a credit system, but the cost seems to vary from about one penny to stream a track to about 20 pence or so to download an expensive CD. The streaming quality is less than hi-fi, and you only get to hear the material once. Downloading provides better technical quality and there seems to be no limit on the number of times each track or CD can be played. However, bear in mind that the downloaded material can not be copied to a CD or used on another computer.

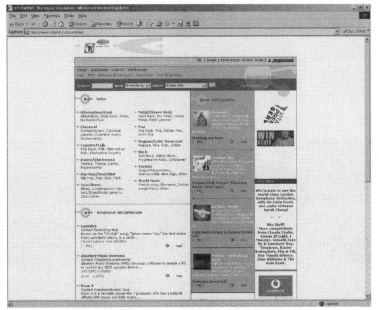

Fig.2.65   The homepage of Vitaminic.co.uk

A wide range of musical tastes are catered for. Pop, classical, jazz, easy listening, etc., are all available, and in substantial quantities. Unfortunately, the high cost of burning CDs will probably deter many would-be users of this site.

This is another general music site that is worth a visit:

www.vitaminic.co.uk

Figure 2.65 shows the homepage, and the links in the top left-hand section of the page enable various types of music to be accessed. Figure 2.66 shows the section for jazz and blues music. There is also a useful search facility. You can subscribe to this site, and a pay per download system is available. There is a certain

125

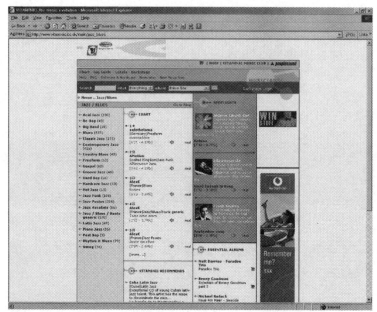

Fig.2.66 The section for jazz and blues music

amount of free content available as well, and it is well worth delving into this site to see what you can find.

At the time of writing this, Microsoft has just launched a new music site at:

http://www.windowsmedia.com

This seems to offer large amounts of free music and other material in streamed form. The material is provided by other sites and each piece of streamed audio or video is accompanied by a pop-up advertisement for the site concerned. There is a search facility near the top of the homepage (Figure 2.67), and this provides an easy way to track down all

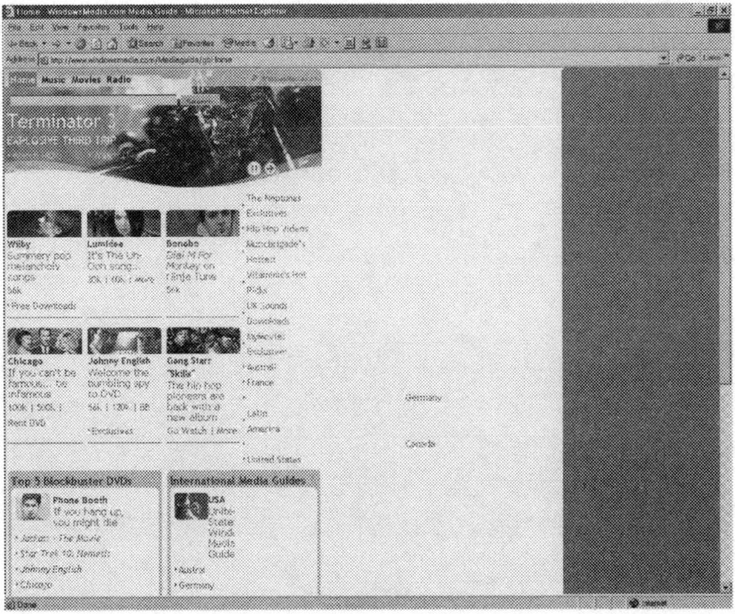

Fig.2.67 A search facility is available

sorts of music. It is certainly worth paying this site a visit.

There are many other legitimate music sites on the Internet, and these are some you might like to visit:

www.mp3.com

www.dotmusic.com

www.freeserve.com/musicclub

www.ministryofsound.com

www.mtv.com/music/downloads

www.pressplay.com

www.wippit.com

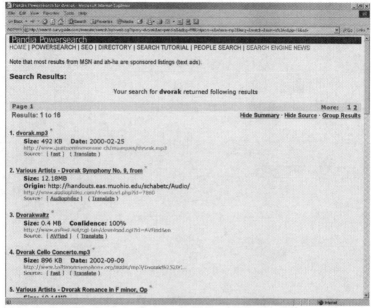

Fig.2.68 The search results for "Dvorak"

Note that most of these have a strong bias to contemporary pop, rock, etc. There are numerous small sites offering music from up and coming bands, amateur orchestras and ensembles, and so on. A good search engine will probably produce some interesting sites, but it will also spew out the addresses of thousands that are not worth visiting. Many of these will be decidedly dodgy, so proceed with caution if you use a search engine to go in search of music on the Internet.

Some search engines have facilities specifically for searching for MP3 music files, and the Pandia search engine mentioned previously has an MP3 option in

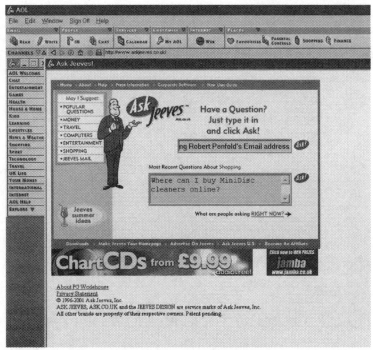

Fig.2.69 First ask "Jeeves" a question

the Select menu. Figure 2.68 shows the result of using "Dvorak" as the search word. This has produced a number of matches, but some of the files proved to be inaccessible. Nevertheless, there were some useful results in the list, and a specialist MP3 search facility is probably the best way of trawling the Internet for MP3 files.

People

Finding people is another specialist area where the general search method might not work very well. It

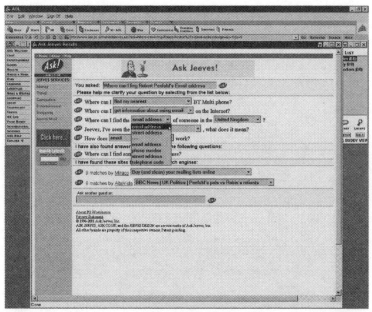

Fig.2.70 You are next presented with some options

works well if you are looking for information about someone who is even slightly famous (or infamous). There is bound to be some information about them on the world's web sites, and any good search engine should find those sites for you. It works less well when you are looking for a long lost relative, friend, or colleague. The search should find them provided they have a web site, which will presumably include their name. It will also find some information about them if their name appears on other web sites for some reason. With most people though, this method will not provide anything useful.

One way of searching for people is to go to the AskJeeves.co.uk site and type in a question along the

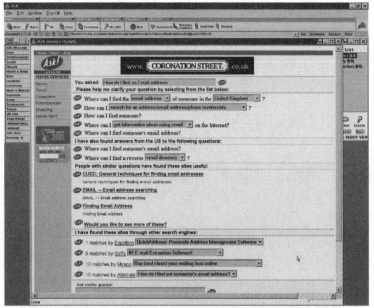

Fig.2.71 More search methods are offered here

lines "How do I find so-and-so's Email address?" (Figure 2.69). You will then be presented with a selection of questions to ask (Figure 2.70), and in this case we require the one that enables a search to be made for the Email address of someone in the UK. Note though, that the drop-down menu gives alternatives to searching for an Email address, such as looking for a street address or a telephone number. Similarly, via another menu you can search for someone outside the UK.

An alternative approach with the AskJeeves web site is to ask a general question about finding an Email address, such as "How can I find someone?" This

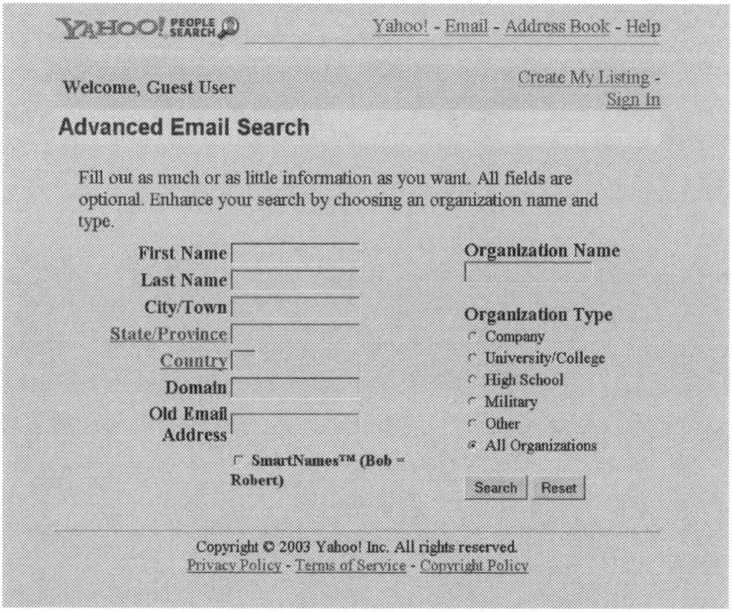

Fig.2.72 The Yahoo! Advanced Email Search

should produce a page something like the one in Figure 2.71. One of the options is the same as before, but there are others that provide more information about the techniques that can be used to locate someone. It also gives an option that helps you to find a reverse Email directory. With a directory of this type you provide an Email address and it tries to find the name of the address's owner.

Yahoo!

The Yahoo search engine includes one or two facilities for locating people, but they can be a bit difficult to track down. In the Email section there is an Advanced

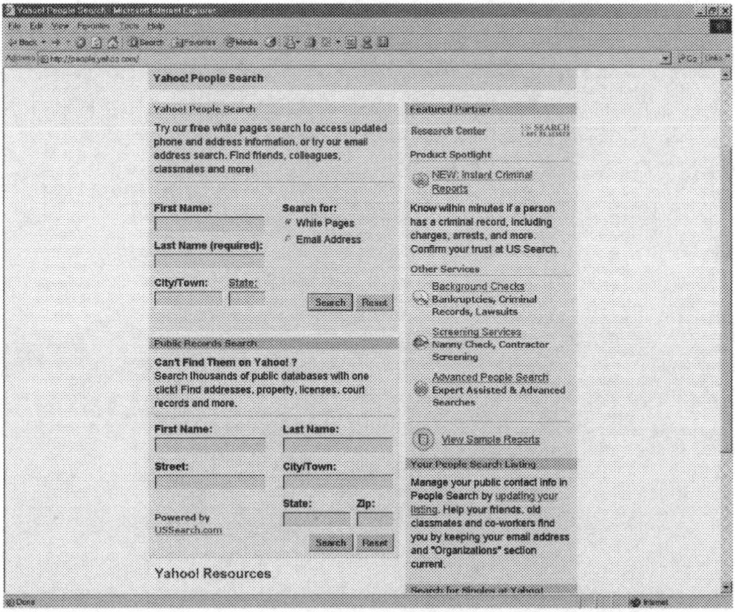

Fig.2.73 Further searching facilities at Yahoo!

Email Search facility (Figure 2.72) where you can enter a name and country, and the search facility will then look for people that match your search criteria. If you go to the Yahoo.com website and activate the "People Search" link, the page of Figure 2.73 will appear. This offers some search facilities, together with links to further search facilities, but it is only designed for locating people resident in the USA. At one time there was a "People Search" link on the Yahoo! UK and Ireland site, but this feature seems to have been discontinued.

There is a useful People Search facility provided by 192.com (www.192.com). Going to the 192.com site

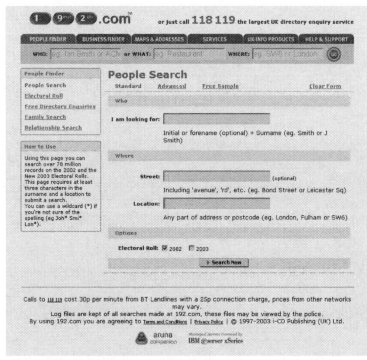

Fig.2.74 The People Search facility at 192.com

and operating the "People Search" link produces the page of Figure 2.74. Here the name of the person you are searching for is added into the top textbox. The other two textboxes are used to indicate the area in which the person lives. Unfortunately, it seems that there is no longer a limited free service on offer, so it is necessary to buy some credits before a search can be carried out.

There is a "People Search" link on the homepage of the Pandia search engine, or you can go direct to the

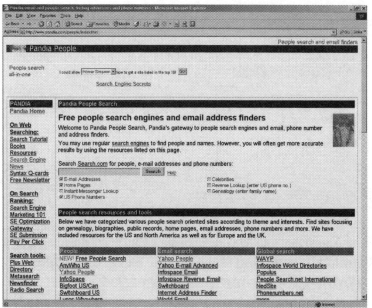

Fig.2.75 Searching for people at Pandia.com

page at this address:

http://www.pandia.com/people/index.html

This page (Figure 2.75) includes a search facility, and it also includes a number of links to other sites that include facilities for finding people.

Postcode/address

The Post Office has a useful site at:

www.postoffice.co.uk

As one would expect, this has sections that give the current postage rates within the UK and for sending mail overseas, general advice on mailing items, and

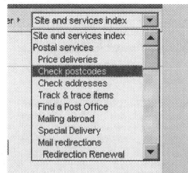

Fig.2.76 The Service menu

so on. There are also excellent postcode and address finding facilities. These can be accessed via the menu near the top right-hand corner of the homepage (Figure 2.76). In order to use either of these facilities it is necessary to register with the site first, but this is a very simple process. You just have to supply a nickname, Email address, and a password. You are only allowed eight searches within a 24 hour period.

These facilities are very useful if you have a partially legible name and address. With the postcode finder you supply the house name or number, the street, and the town (Figure 2.77). The search then produces the

Fig.2.77 The form used for finding postcodes

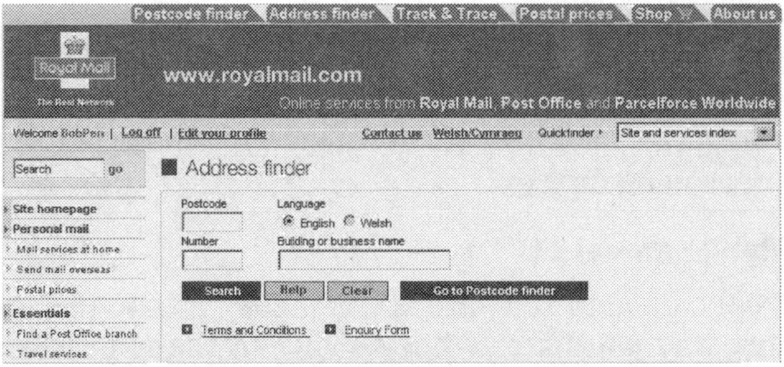

Fig.2.78 The form for finding addresses

appropriate postcode. In the case of the address finder (Figure 2.78) you must supply the postcode and the house name or number. If the search is successful it will produce the rest of the address. If no house name or number is supplied, the search produces a list of all the addresses that match the supplied postcode.

Software

If you need top quality items of major software you have to pay the price, which is often quite high. You can actually download some normal commercial software and pay online by credit card. This facility is offered by some of the large online computer stores, and in a few cases it is also available from the software publisher's site. Often there is a discount for buying in this way, but there is the drawback that you do not get a ready-made CD containing the software or any printed documentation.

Probably of more interest to most computer users is the cheap or free software that is available for download. This falls into about half a dozen main categories, and it is worth considering these before proceeding further.

Public domain (PD)

Public domain software is completely free to use in any way you like. Whoever owned the copyright originally has decided to let it lapse and relinquish all rights to the software.

Freeware

This seems to be a modern term for public domain software. However, some software that claims to be in this category is free for you to use, but there are restrictions on its commercial use or redistribution. This is unlikely to matter to most users, but it is as well to read the "fine print".

Open source

This is similar to public domain and freeware. It is free to use, and programmers can even alter programs of use part of the program code in their own projects. There may be some "strings attached", but these normally apply only to those wishing to alter the programs or use parts of them in their own programs.

Shareware

Most downloadable programs fall into this category. The exact way the system operates varies from one program to another. In some cases the software that you download is the fully operational "real thing". You are allowed to use it without charge for a certain period of time, which is usually about 30 days. Thereafter you are expected to either remove it from your computer or pay for it. If you are dishonest, it can be left on your PC and it will continue to work normally.

These days most of the programs are fully operational, but only for a trial period that is usually between about 15 and 30 days. An alternative approach is to have a limit on the number of times that the program can be launched. Either way, the program is unusable once the limit has been reached, and reinstalling the software will not get it working again. It can be reactivated by paying the appropriate fee and following the instructions that will then be supplied by the software publisher.

In a few cases the downloaded software is not fully working. With a word processor for instance, you might only be able to have a hundred words per document. Alternatively, some functions of the program are omitted. Programs of this type are called "crippled" programs, and are probably not worth downloading. It is not possible to properly assess programs that have major features missing or will only permit tiny amounts of data to be used.

Trial programs

Trial programs are essentially the same as shareware, and they are programs that will only work for a certain period of time. These days the majority of trial programs are complete and fully functional, but might lack some of the extras such as clipart and utilities that are supplied with the commercial version of the program. Trial software differs from the shareware variety in that there is normally no option to pay a fee and make the program fully operational. Instead you have to buy the program in the normal way, uninstall the trial software, and then install the commercial version.

You will probably encounter references to "demo" (demonstration) programs, and this term is often used as an alternative name for trial software. However, in some cases it is software that provides a running demonstration that describes the features of software and shows you how to use them. Running demonstrations are undoubtedly useful for showing you how to use software and showing the features that are available, but are not proper substitutes for fully operational programs that you can try for yourself. I would definitely advise against buying software on the strength of an impressive running demonstration alone.

Finding software

If you are interested in a specific program, using the name of the program in a search engine should provide some useful links. If you would like to go in search of shareware and freeware programs in general, there are sites that specialise in searching

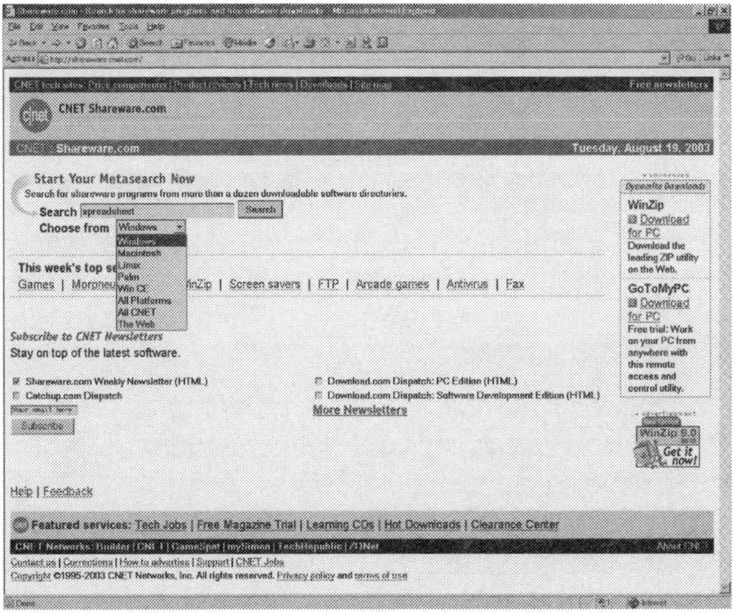

Fig.2.79 The Shareware.com homepage

for these types of software. One of the most popular is:

www.shareware.com

Despite its name, it does provide links to other types of software including freeware and some commercial trial programs. The homepage (Figure 2.79) has a search facility, but you must select the appropriate operating system from the menu before starting a search. In most cases the default (Windows) will be the one that you need, but it is possible to search for software that runs under other operating systems such as Linux and those used on Macintosh computers.

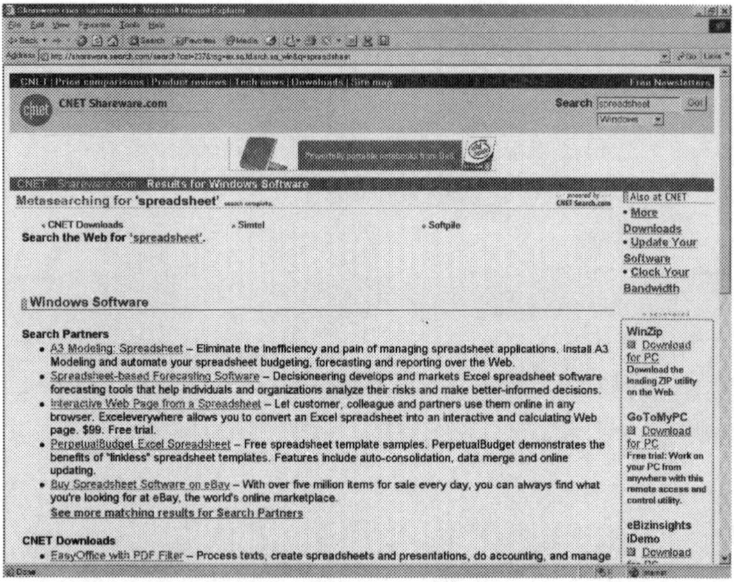

Fig.2.80 The search results for "spreadsheet"

In Figure 2.80 the word "spreadsheet" was used as the search string, and a scrollable list of results from various sources has been produced. The list includes spreadsheet programs and add-ons for popular software of this type. You can search for programs by name, and Figure 2.81 shows the result of searching for the popular ZoneAlarm firewall program. Links to several versions of the program have been found.

Another useful software search facility is available at:

www.download.com

Figure 2.82 shows the homepage for this site, and the search facility is in the top right-hand section of the

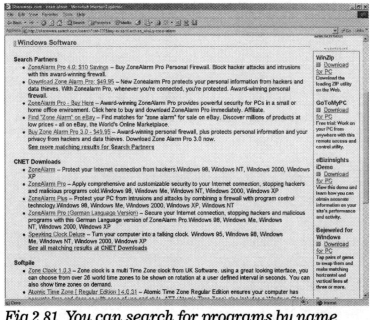

Fig.2.81 You can search for programs by name

page. This site offers an alternative approach in the form of a directory system. Figure 2.83 shows the result of operating the "Internet" link. The upper section of the page provides links to various subcategories, and these are also directly available from the homepage. The lower

Fig.2.82 Download.com

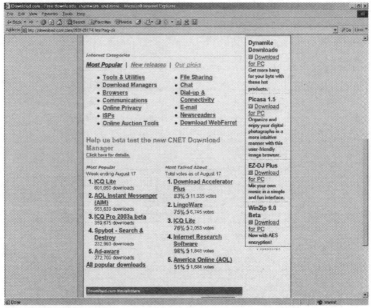

Fig.2.83 Download.com includes a directory

section lists the most popular programs in the general category that was selected. Left-clicking a subcategory produces a list of programs (Figure 2.84).

In order to download a program it is necessary to first left-click its entry in the list. This will take you to a page that provides more information about the program, and in most cases there is a link to the publisher's web site. There will also be a "Download" or "Download Now" link. Usually it is merely necessary to left-click this link in order to make the File Download window appear (Figure 2.85). If this fails to have the desired effect it might be necessary

98/Me/NT/2000/XP File Size: 1.16MB License: Free to try, $49 to buy					
CT Cookie Spy 2.0 Get rid of spying cookies. OS: Windows 95/98/NT/2000 File Size: 137.51K License: Free	01/03/2001	81% 26 votes		27,261	Download now
Webwasher 2.21 Remove unwanted ads from your downloads. OS: Windows 95/98/NT/2000 File Size: 993.27K License: Free	01/08/2001	75% 209 votes		91,000	Download now
PGP-ICQ 0.95 Encrypt your ICQ messages with this privacy utility. OS: Windows 95/98/NT/2000 File Size: 1.66MB License: Free	02/06/2001	83% 12 votes		17,882	Download now
PGPfreeware 8.0.2 Protect your e-mail from unauthorized viewing. OS: Windows (all) File Size: 8.44MB License: Free	02/20/2001	57% 255 votes		364,833	Download now
Re-sort by Name	Date added	User rating	Editorial rating How we rate	Downloads Total	Last week	Availability

Fig.2.84 Left-click a category to produce a program list

to right-click on the link and then select Save Target As from the pop-up menu.

If this fails to work properly and you just get error messages, it is likely that the link to the file is "dead". Note that sites like Download.com do not normally have the program files stored on their own site. They are simply providing links to files stored on other sites. If the link does not work it is possible that you will

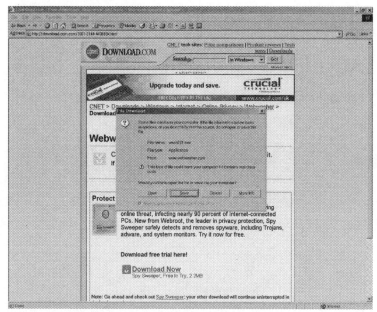

Fig.2.85 The File Download window

have better luck if you go to the publisher's web site and look for a link there. The link to the file on the publisher's web site should be up-to-date and (hopefully) working. If you can not get any of the links to a file to work properly it might be worthwhile trying later in the day, or a day or two later. A fair proportion of shareware is not successful and simply disappears, so some programs will simply not be available any more.

Assuming that the Save File window does appear, operate the Save button. The usual Windows file browser will then appear (Figure 2.86) so that a destination for the file can be selected. You can just

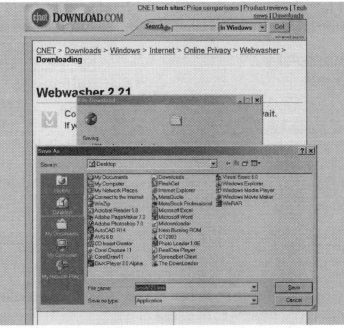

Fig.2.86 The usual file browser appears next

settle for the default folder, but I would recommend making a folder specifically for downloading program files unless you only intend to download one or two programs. The text in the "File name" field can be altered if you wish, but do not alter the extension (the three letters to the right of the full stop). These indicate the file type to Windows and certain applications.

Operate the Save button to go ahead and download the file. A window like the one shown in Figure 2.87 will show how well (or otherwise) that the download is progressing. The time taken depends on a number of factors including the size of the file, the speed of your Internet connection, and the speed of the server supplying the file. Progress is unlikely to be more than about one megabyte every three or four minutes when using a 56k connection. Much higher speeds are

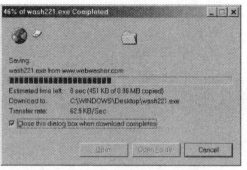

Fig.2.87 The progress window

possible with a broadband connection, but will only be achieved if the server is fast and is not dealing with large numbers of users.

Download times

Large program files of 100 megabytes will often take about half an hour using a broadband connection, but would be more likely to take five or six hours with an ordinary dialup connection. Either way, large downloads require patience. If something goes wrong during the download it might be possible to left-click the download link and resume the download from where you left off. However, this will usually result in the download starting from scratch.

There are programs called download managers that try to optimise the download speed and will also, where possible, resume broken downloads. FlashGet and Download Accelerator Plus are two popular programs of this type. You will certainly need a download manager if you wish to download large programs using an Internet connection that cuts off after you have been on the Internet for an hour or two.

Once the file has been downloaded it can be installed. This is most easily achieved where the downloaded file has an "exe" extension to the filename. This indicates that it is an executable program file, and running it should start a normal Windows style installation process. Probably the easiest way of running an executable file is to locate it using Windows Explorer and then double-click on its entry or icon.

Some programs are supplied as compressed archives. In other words, the files needed for installation have been compressed into one file that was made as small as possible so that it downloads relatively quickly. In fact some executable files are compressed archives. Running a file of this type causes the archive to be decompressed and stored on the computer's hard disc drive. In most cases though, a decompression program will be needed, such as the popular WinZip program that is used for decompressing files having a "zip" extension. Decompression programs are available from sites such as Download.com.

Risks

If you were to design a system that would make it easy for viruses and other computer "nasties" to spread around the world as quickly and efficiently as possible, you would probably end up with something very similar to the Internet. Computer viruses can be spread in other ways, and it is important not to overlook this fact, but the Internet has become synonymous with computer viruses. If you are going to download files via the Internet you need to be aware of the risks and should take the appropriate precautions.

There is actually a variety of program types that can attack a computer system and damage files on any accessible disc drive. These tend to be lumped together under the term "virus", but strictly speaking a virus is a parasitic program that can reproduce itself and spread across a system, or from one system to another. A virus attaches itself to other programs, but it is not immediately apparent to the user that anything has happened. A virus can be benign, but usually it starts to do serious damage at some stage, and will often infect the boot sector of the hard disc, rendering the system unbootable.

It can also affect the FAT (file allocation table) of a disc so that the computer can not find some of the files stored on the disc. The disc can be attacked in other ways, and it might even be rendered totally inaccessible. The less subtle viruses take more direct action such as attempting to erase or overwrite everything on the hard disc, or erasing the system files while flashing an abusive message on the screen.

A virus can be spread from one computer to another via an infected file, which can enter the second computer via a disc, a modem, or over a network, which includes the Internet. In fact any means of transferring a file from one computer to another is a potential route for spreading viruses. A program is really only a virus if it attaches itself to other programs and replicates itself.

A program is not a virus if it is put forward as a useful applications program but it actually starts damaging the system when it is run. This type of program is more correctly called a "Trojan Horse" or just a "Trojan". Another form of Trojan is the "backdoor" variety. This makes it easier for hackers to access your PC, and perhaps steal important information from it.

Virus protection

This is a case where the old adage of "prevention is better than cure" certainly applies. There is probably a cure for every computer virus, but identifying and eradicating a virus can take a great deal of time. Also, having removed the virus there is no guarantee that all your files will still be intact. In fact there is a very good chance that some damage will have been done. In a worst case scenario there may be no choice but to reformat the hard disc and reinstall the operating system and all the applications software. It might be possible to rescue some of your data from the disc prior to reformatting the disc, but all the data could be lost.

Most anti-virus programs will run in the background and automatically check any newly downloaded file

2 Specialist searches

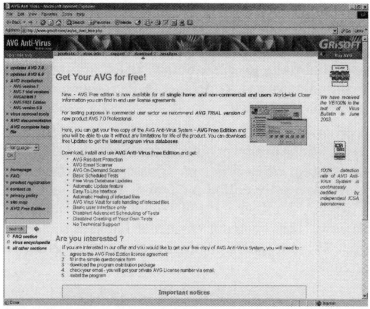

Fig.2.88 The Grisoft homepage

for viruses. In fact most will automatically check any new file, including those on CD-ROMs, etc. Some even check for things like malicious scripts in pages that are downloaded via the Internet. These scripts try to do things like changing your browser's default homepage (the page that loads each time you launch the browser), or other settings.

There are plenty of commercial anti-virus programs available, but there are also one or two really good free anti-virus programs. It is certainly worth visiting the Grisoft web site at:

www.grisoft.com

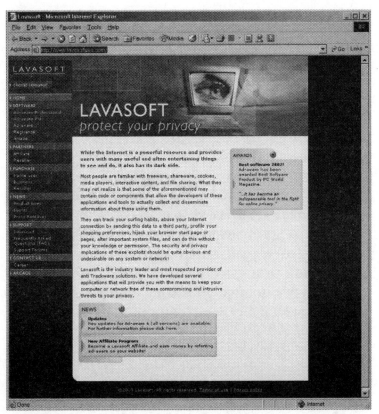

Fig.2.89 Lavasoft produce the Ad Aware program

On the home page there should be a link in the list down the left-hand side called something like "AVG Free Edition". Activating this link will bring up a page like the one in Figure 2.88. This gives some information about the free version of the AVG antivirus program and provides a link that enables it to be downloaded. You do have to go through a registration process, but it is worth the effort. Anti-virus programs soon become out of date, but monthly updates to AVG are available free of charge. It has a reputation for being very efficient, and it certainly detected a couple of backdoor Trojan programs on my system that a certain well known commercial program had failed to detect. It is one of the best freebies on the Internet.

Another useful freebie is the standard version of Ad Aware, which is a program designed to locate and (if required) remove "spy-ware". This type of software is not usually as risky as viruses and Trojans, but most regard it as an invasion of privacy. Spy-ware would typically track your surfing habits and send this information to a third party. Some spy-ware also changes your homepage setting, and possibly other Internet settings of your computer. The freeware version of Ad Aware is available from this site, together with more information on the program and spy-ware:

www.lavasoftusa.com

Point to remember

It is possible to search successfully for most things using an ordinary search engine, but with some types of search there are better methods, such as using a specialist search engine or database.

There are many sites that offer music that you can download and play using the Windows Media Player that is supplied with Windows. However, few of these sites operate legally. The sites that are legal will often require a subscription or other payment for the music that you download.

Music videos are also available, but most of these can only be streamed if you have some form of fast Internet connection. Some can be played on the Windows Media Player but others require the free Real One Player to be downloaded and installed.

There are many Internet radio stations around the world covering jazz, classical music, pop music, financial news, and many other topics. The audio quality provided by most of these stations is fine for speech, but the quality of music is often a trifle disappointing.

Internet television stations are also available, but few seem to provide "live" streaming. Most provide a selection of recorded programs that can be streamed, but they can still be useful and interesting. A broadband Internet connection and fast streaming are needed to produce something approaching normal television quality.

In order to find people, addresses, telephone numbers, etc., it is usually necessary to use specialist search engines and databases. Many of these are only of use when looking for people living in North America. There are good services of this type for the UK, but these days they are not usually free.

It is possible to download many types of software via the Internet. Some of this software is genuinely free, but most of it is limited in some way such as only operating for a certain number of days. There is some good free software though, and it can be fun to try out different types of software.

When downloading anything, but particularly when downloading programs, take due care not to introduce any malicious programs into your PC. There are free anti-virus programs and other software that will keep your PC free from viruses, Trojans, etc. If you do not use this software, or a commercial equivalent, you will probably regret it.

Just for us

Wrong generation?

There is perhaps a general perception that the Internet is for the young, and that it offers little for those who have reached thirty something or more. I think it is fair to say that there is probably more on the Internet for youngsters than for the older generations, but the quantity of information on the Internet is now so great that there is certainly something for everyone. The percentage aimed specifically at the older generation is not large, but it is still substantial in absolute terms. By necessity, many of the sites are country-specific. If you need to know about UK benefits there is no point in looking at sites in the USA or Australia.

Even so, there are still plenty of sites that are of interest to over 50s in the UK. Of course, a web site is of interest to people of most ages if they are interested in the topics covered by the site. For example, a good site on photography is of interest to photographers of all ages. This chapter is concerned with sites specifically for those over 50, and sites that have a large content of particular interest to this age group. General sites that are likely to be of interest to many people over 50 are covered in subsequent chapters.

Age Concern (www.ageconcern.co.uk)

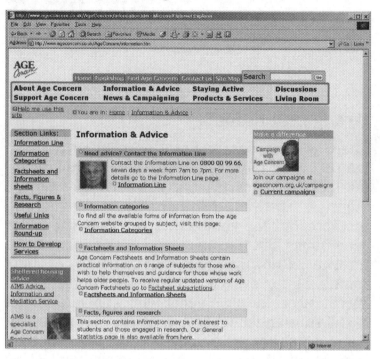

I would guess that Age Concern is the biggest and best known UK organisation that campaigns for the rights of the elderly. It also provides numerous leaflets giving advice on matters such as housing, heath, and benefits. These can be requested via their site or you can download them in Adobe PDF format. Many documents on the Internet are now provided in this format, and you need to have the reader program installed on your PC in order to view them.

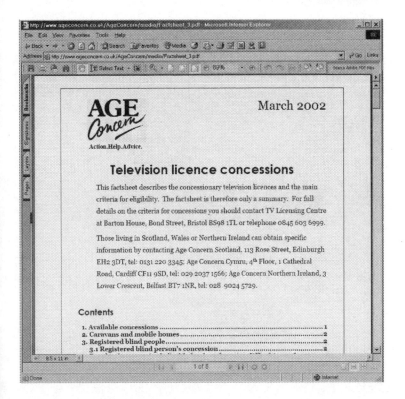

Fortunately, the Acrobat Reader program can be downloaded free of charge from Adobe's web site, and a link to the download page is provided wherever PDF documents are offered. The documents can be printed out from the reader program if your PC is equipped with a suitable printer. In addition to the leaflets, there are some useful links on the Age Concern site, together with information about the organisation itself.

Its official (www.over50.gov.uk)

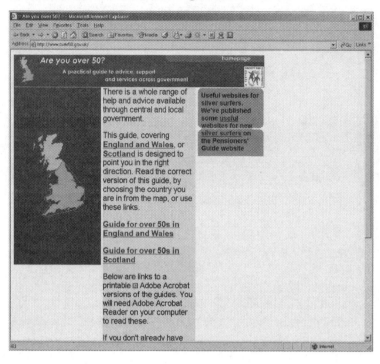

This is the official government site for the over 50s.
It is effectively two sites, with separate sections for
Scotland and England/Wales. There does not seem
to be a section for Northern Ireland. There are guides
in PDF format and some links to other sites for the
over 50s.

Pensions (www.info4pensioners.gov.uk)

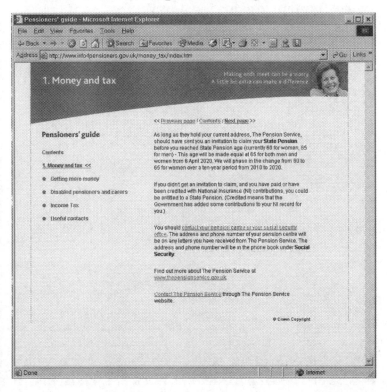

Another government site, and as the name suggests, it provides information for pensioners. It provides information about a range of topics such as money and tax, bereavement, learning, travel, and leisure. The amount of information on each topic is not that large, and it is primarily aimed at helping you determine what is and is not applicable to your situation. There are links to other sites that provide more information if you need it.

Pensions Service
(www.thepensionservice.gov.uk)

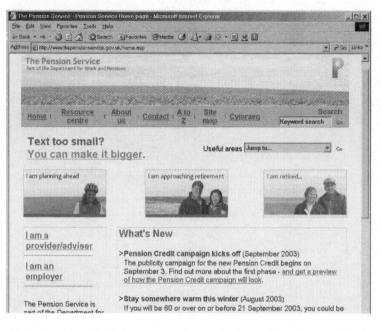

This is the official site of The Pensions Service, which is part of The Department of Work and Pensions. It contains advice for those planning well ahead, those approaching retirement, and those already in retirement. It provides a large amount of general information about the way in which the pension system operates, how to make claims, etc. Note that like the other government sites it only provides general information about the way in which things operate. There is no financial advice in the normally accepted sense of the term. With something as complex as pensions you may need expert advice from a financial advisor on some aspects of things.

Government directory (www.ukonline.gov.uk)

Not really a site for the over 50s, but one that it is well worth knowing about. It is effectively a search engine and directory for government web sites. It includes local government sites as well as government departments. If a government department of any type has a web site, then it should be listed here. I managed to find my local council's site in about ten seconds.

Seniors Network (www.seniorsnetwork.co.uk)

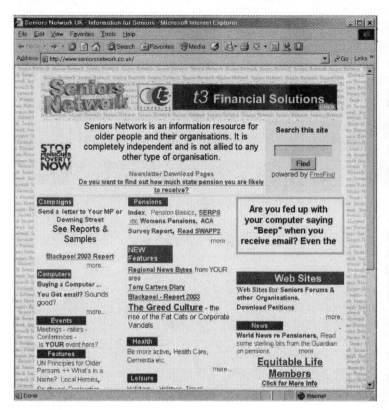

The Seniors Network site is an independent site that describes itself as an "information resource". This it certainly is, and it contains information on a very wide range of topics. It seems to be a sort of "rough guide" to being a senior citizen, and it definitely does not take a "rose coloured glasses" approach to things. This is a very useful and interesting web site.

50 Connect (www.50connect.co.uk)

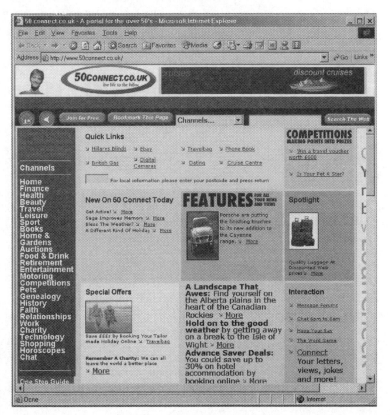

If the sites covered so far are a bit on the heavy side for you, this one should be "more up your street". It is an online magazine that has articles covering subjects such as holidays, health, gardening, and finance. There is also a forum where you can discuss your interests with others. You have to join in order to access some features of the site, but registration is free.

IDF50 (www.idf50.co.uk)

Another light-hearted site, its full title is "I Don't Feel 50". Amongst other things, it has articles on travel, computers, health, poetry, and work, together with forums. It has been around since 1997, which in Internet terms makes it at least as old as its target audience!

Laterlife (www.laterlife.co.uk)

Another general site aimed at those aged 50 or more. There is a useful "welcome" page that gives information about the purpose of the site, and a site map that helps you to find specific features. There are some guides and articles, but the site is more commercially oriented than the other sites featured here. Of course, if you are looking for a handyman or a holiday this would probably be considered an advantage.

Over 50s (www.over50s.com)

This is yet another general site for the over 50s, covering the usual mix of news, health, travel, home, garden, etc. There is also a useful legal section with advice about making a will, dealing with age discrimination, etc. It is a very professionally produced site.

Retirement Matters
(www.retirement-matters.co.uk)

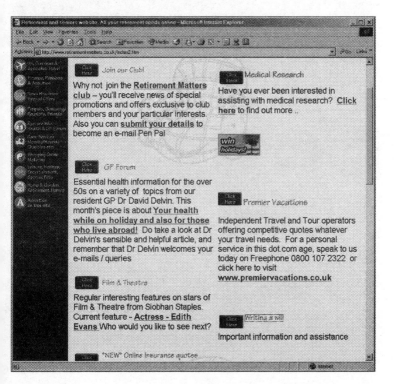

This site includes some useful information, including quite a large article on making a will. It also has a large number of links to sites covering subjects such as genealogy, bereavement, and mobility.

NIACE (www.niace.org.uk)

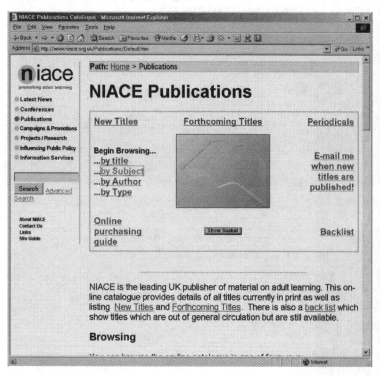

If you are interested in adult education, the web site of your local authority, and nearby authorities, should have details of the courses they offer, or information about obtaining these details. General information about adult education can be found at the NIACE (The National Institute of Adult Continuing Education) site. Various publications are offered by this site and there is a useful search facility.

City & Guilds (www.timetolearn.org.uk)

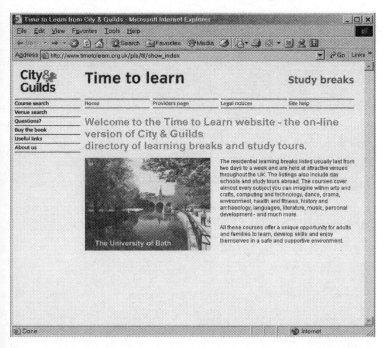

The "Time to Learn" site is the online version of the City & Guilds directory of learning breaks and study tours. In other words, it is a directory of holidays where you go somewhere nice to learn to paint, or go on a tour to learn more about certain places. There are search facilities that will produce a list of (say) all the art courses situated in the south west of England. There is also a useful list of links to other adult education related sites. If you are really serious about education there is the Open University site (www.open.ac.uk). The elderly apparently have a high level of success with the Open University.

3   Just for us

Wise Owls (www.wiseowls.co.uk)

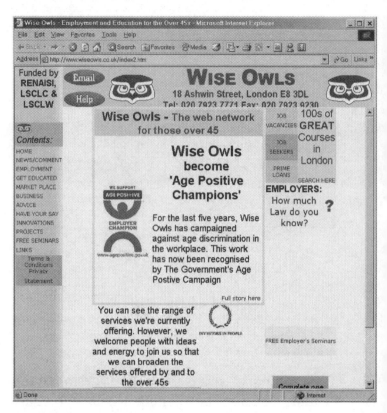

Wise Owls is an organisation that campaigns against age discrimination in the workplace. It carries a certain amount of news and comment, but much of the site actually seems to be devoted to adult education, with particular emphasis on courses for those over the age of 45.

Bereavement Register
www.the-bereavement-register.org.uk/uk/)

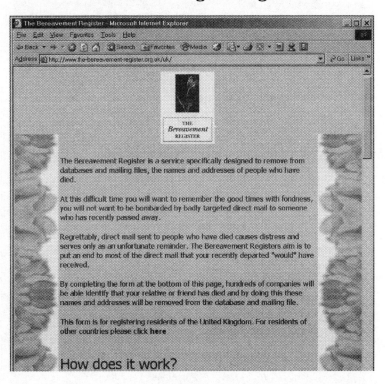

These days most people are on numerous databases and mailing lists. It can be very upsetting to keep receiving mail for deceased relatives, even if it is only junk mail. Unfortunately, this is something that can continue for several years. The Bereavement Register provides a free service that helps to remove deceased persons from databases and mailing lists. It is unlikely to be 100 percent effective, but it should greatly reduce the amount of distressing mail received.

WidowNet (www.fortnet.org/WidowNet)

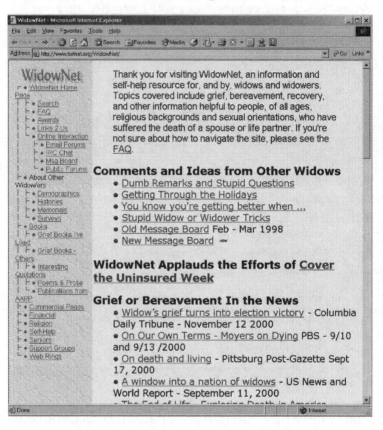

WidowNet is written for and by widows and widowers. It deals in a direct manner with awkward issues, and provides an online forum. This site is based in the USA, but much of the content is equally applicable to the UK.

Saga Magazine (www.saga.co.uk/magazine)

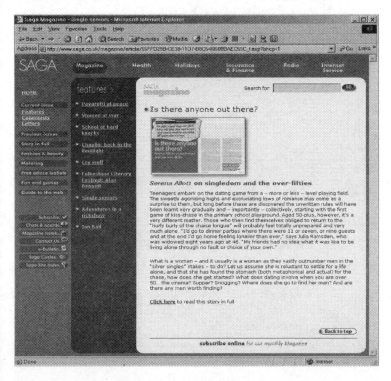

Saga is synonymous with the 50 plus age group, and it is a company that is well known for its insurance, holidays, and other services. I suppose that many of us considered ourselves to be official "wrinklies" when we qualified to buy Saga products. Saga publishes a magazine, and it is also available online. It is possible to access back issues as well. There is an interesting mix of articles, and the magazine is not just a disguised advertisement for Saga products. As far as I can see, there is no charge for the online version of the magazine.

Retirement Site
(www.the-retirement-site.co.uk)

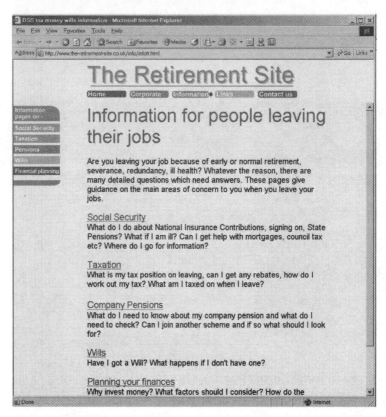

The Retirement Site seems to be aimed at those approaching retirement rather than those who have already retired. If you are approaching retirement, or have recently retired, you will probably find answers to a lot of questions at this site.

ARP (www.arp050.org.uk)

ARP (Association of Retired Persons) describes itself as the leading campaigning and social organisation for those over the age of 50. It is necessary to join this organisation in order to gain access to all its facilities, but there is a lot of information available via the "HELP SECTION" link. There seems to be no charge for accessing this information.

Retirement with a purpose
(www.retirementwithapurpose.com)

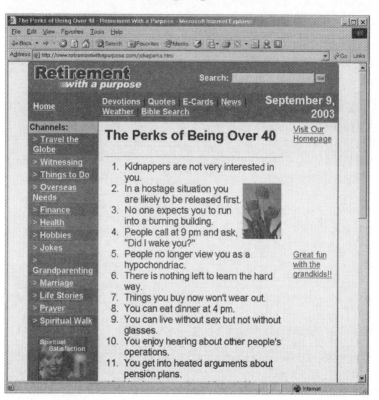

There are plenty of sites for the over 50s that are based outside the UK. These often have plenty of interesting and amusing material, but bear in mind that any sections on such things as pensions, benefits, etc., will not be applicable to those in the UK. This is a Christian site based in the USA, but there is plenty of material of interest to Christians and non-Christians alike.

Hells Geriatrics (www.hellsgeriatrics.co.uk)

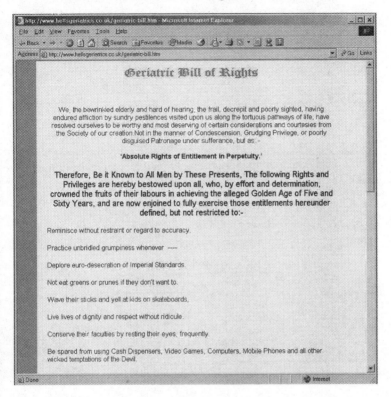

Definitely a site "with attitude" this one. If you have no intention of growing old gracefully, then you will find plenty of interest on this site. There is also a Hells Geriatrics group on Yahoo! where you can correspond with like-minded people. The web has plenty of Monty Python fans, so I was confident there would be a similar site at www.hellsgrannies.com. I was mistaken though, although it will probably turn up in due course.

Help the Aged (www.helptheaged.org.uk)

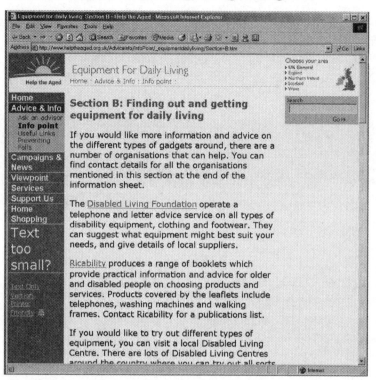

Last, but certainly not least, Help the Aged is a large and well-known organisation that campaigns for the rights of the elderly. Their web site has news about their campaigns and details of fund raising events. It has a new section that provides advice on a range of topics, and there is also a forum where you can post your opinion on the latest contentious issues. There is a section that explains the range of services that Help the Aged provides. Well worth a look if you are in need of help or would like to provide help.

Legal matters

Rights and wrongs

The number of UK sites dealing with legal matters seems to have reduced in recent years. There are still several good legal sites on the Internet, but it has to be pointed out that they are not intended to be a substitute for proper legal advice from a solicitor or lawyer. They are intended more as means of checking your rights. In simple cases this knowledge might be all you need, with the rogue company (or whatever) seeing reason when they realise you know your legal entitlements.

With more complex cases you can check whether you "have a leg to stand on". If it looks as though you need expert advice there are sites that will put you in touch with a solicitor or a lawyer. In the case of consumer rights there are sites that deal specifically with this issue. In fact quite a high proportion of the legal advice on the Internet seems to be devoted to this subject, but there is plenty of advice on other aspects of the law such as housing, employment, and wills.

CAB (www.adviceguide.org.uk)

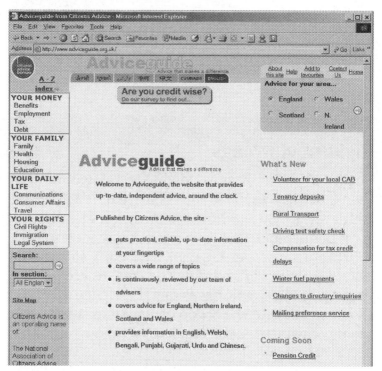

Your local CAB (Citizens Advice Bureau) is a good
place to start if you are having legal difficulties. The
online version of the CAB is called the Advice Guide,
and that nicely sums up its purpose. It covers a wide
range of topics including consumer rights, benefits,
health, housing, education, employment, debt, and
taxation. It is kept up-to-date, and there are versions
for England/Wales, Northern Ireland, and Scotland.
If you decide that a trip to your local CAB is required,
there is a useful search facility that will locate the
CAB offices in your area.

CAB-2 (www.nacab.org.uk)

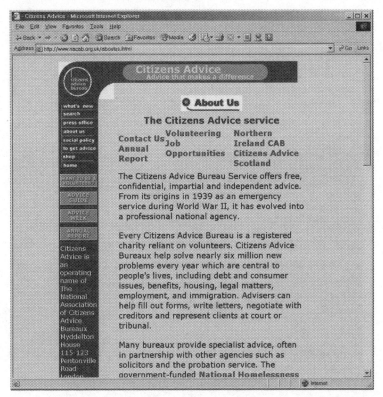

This is the official site of the National Association of Citizen Advice Bureaux, but it is very different to the Advice Guide. It is principally about the organisation itself rather than trying to provide online help. However, this site gives some useful background information on the organisation, information about how to volunteer, and there is a link to the advice guide.

Compact Law (www.compactlaw.co.uk)

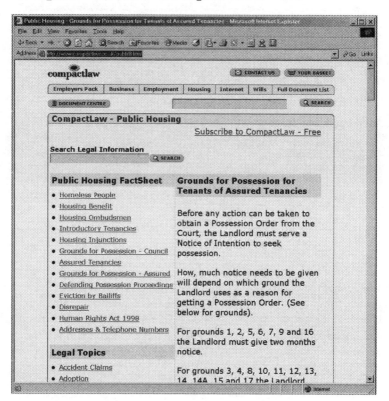

This is a commercial site, but it seems to have a large amount of free information on a good range of subjects including housing and consumer rights. It is perhaps less wide ranging than the Advice Guide site, but those subjects that are covered are covered in some depth.

Click Docs (www.clickdocs.co.uk)

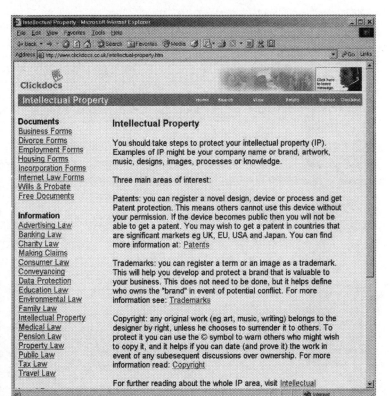

This is another commercial site, and its main purpose is to provide legal documents, such as a will for example, that can be downloaded and customised. I suppose that it is a sort of online version of the forms and help packs that are sold by some stationers. There is also some free information and some useful links to other sites.

TSI (www.tradingstandards.gov.uk)

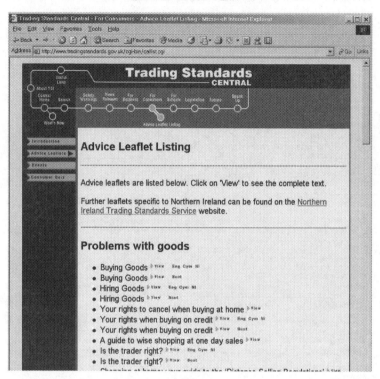

This site is maintained by the TSI (Trading Standards Institute), and it has a number of large sections. The one that is likely to be of primary interest is the Consumer section, which is selected via the link near the top of the homepage. Then select the Advice Leaflets section via the button in the left-hand section of the page. The site includes a huge range of leaflets that can be read online, and most types of product and service are covered, as are your rights when buying on credit, over the Internet, etc. A comprehensive coverage of consumer rights in fact.

Watchdog (www.bbc.co.uk/watchdog)

The BBC's Watchdog programme has its origins back in 1970s where it grew out of the Nationwide programme. Back then it was The Consumer Unit, and this part of the programme was presented by Richard Stilgoe. Watchdog is still going strong and it has a substantial presence on the BBC's web site. As one would expect, there is a substantial amount of advice on offer, including a very useful glossary of legal terms and some guides. You can download Watchdog letters to help you complain about an unsatisfactory holiday, poor workmanship, etc. Definitely a site worth investigating.

Solicitors-Online (www.solicitors-online.com)

The Solicitors-Online site is maintained by the Law Society, and it is a database of the law firms in the UK. It includes a search facility that enables a solicitor to be found by name. Alternatively, you can supply a location and it will provide a list of the nearest one hundred solicitors for that location. Details are available for each company listed. You can also search for a law firm that specialises in a certain aspect of the law (agriculture, fraud, employment, and so on).

Legal Aid (www.legalservices.gov.uk)

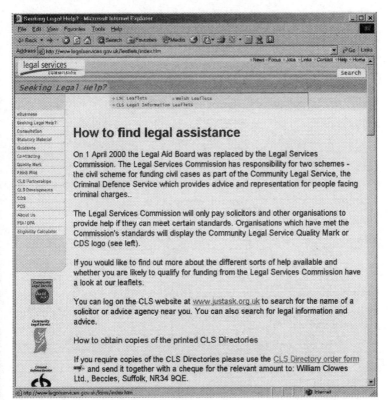

The rules governing legal aid have changed in recent years, and this site has a lot of information about the new rules and regulations. Information leaflets can be ordered from the site or downloaded in printable HTML or Adobe PDF formats. HTML incidentally, is the coding used for ordinary web pages, so the leaflets in this format can be viewed on screen like ordinary web pages. They have no tiny text so they will be easy to read if they are printed.

CJS (www.cjsonline.org)

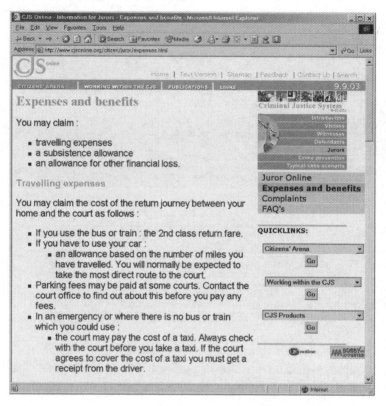

This is a government site that explains and provides general information about the criminal justice system in the UK. There is a great deal of general information about the structure and workings of the criminal justice system. There is also specific information on such things as the rules governing expenses for jurors and crime prevention measures. This is a large site, but a simple menu system makes it easy to navigate what could otherwise be a confusing site.

Financial
sites

Shrinking resources

When the stock markets boomed in the late 1990s, so did Internet sites dealing with stocks and shares in particular and money in general. Like other sites created during the dotcom boom, financial sites found the going very tough when the bubble burst. The largest was UK-Invest, which was originally part of Freeserve, the Internet service provider (ISP). This site is now long gone, as is the UK version of The Street and some of the other top sites.

This is not to say that there is a shortage of money related sites. The amount of information available is probably less that it was at the peak of the dotcom boom, but there was inevitably a lot of duplication between sites. The amount of unique information lost when each site disappeared was probably quite small. In the early days practically all the information was free, but some of it is now only available on subscription. There are still plenty of good financial sites out there. Some of the originals have survived, and a few have actually expanded. One or two new financial sites have appeared. Whether you need information on insurance, funds, shares, loans, or any other financial topic, there will be a few good sites that tell you everything you need to know.

5 Financial sites

Find (www.find.co.uk)

The Find.co.uk name suggests that this is a general search engine, but it is specifically for finding financial products. There is a search facility in the top right-hand corner of the page. Products are placed in ten groups, with each group having a number of subcategories. For example, one product group is headed "Insurance", and this has subcategories such as car and home insurance. Each subcategory contains lists of companies that provide the selected service, together with brief details of each company. Operating a link for one of the companies takes you to the relevant web site. This is a simple and straightforward site that is comprehensive and easy to use.

Ukfind (www.ukfind.biz)

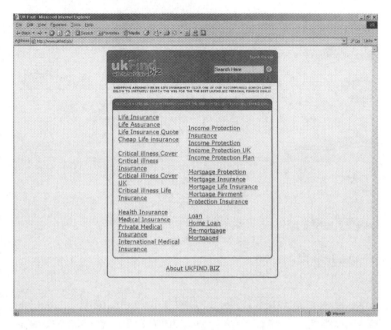

Find.co.uk is probably the biggest financial directory site, but there are others. Ukfind.biz has one of the most basic homepages you will encounter, but it is none the worse for that. Like Find.co.uk, it has a search facility but it is primarily intended to act as a directory for financial web sites. It is much more limited in its scope though, and it only covers insurance and mortgages. The coverage within these fields is pretty impressive though. There are no best buys categories or facilities for finding best buys. If you are after insurance this site could be worth a look.

5   Financial sites

Unbiased (www.unbiased.co.uk)

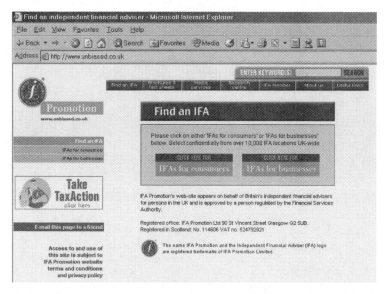

This site is owned by the UK's independent financial advisors, and its primary purpose is to enable private individuals and businesses to find a local advisor. On the homepage you select the consumer or business option, and then on the next page you supply your postcode and choose from certain criteria such as your area of interest (ISAs, equity release, etc.). Next the Find IFA button is operated, and a list of six IFAs is provided. These are the six IFAs that are geographically closest to the supplied postcode and that meet your criteria. Telephone and fax numbers are provided for each IFA, together with an Email address and link to their web site where applicable. If you need the services of a financial advisor I suppose that this is the obvious starting point that could avoid wasted calls.

FSA (www.fsa.gov.uk)

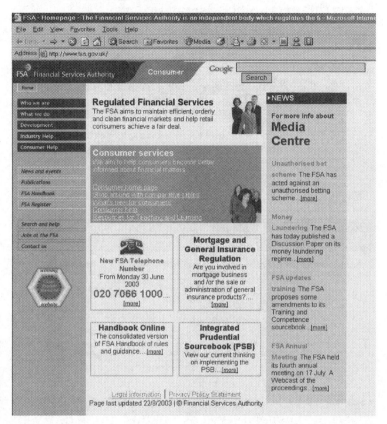

Until recently there were several government organisations overseeing financial services in the UK. Now practically everything financial is governed by the FSA (Financial Services Authority). If you have a complaint about a financial company or simply require more information about the rules and regulations, you will probably find the information you require on this site.

Financial Ombudsman
(www.financial-ombudsman.org.uk)

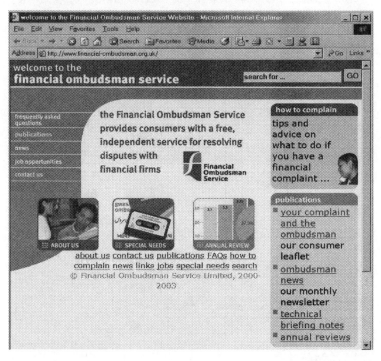

The FSA is responsible for enforcing the rules governing financial services, but they do not deal with disputes between individuals and companies. That is the role of the Financial Ombudsman Service. This website has a lot of information about the financial rules and regulations, and how to pursue complaints. There are online publications that can be downloaded, including one that explains how to make a complaint. The publications are available in several languages. The services of the Financial Ombudsman are free incidentally.

Scams (www.fsa.gov.uk/consumer/scams)

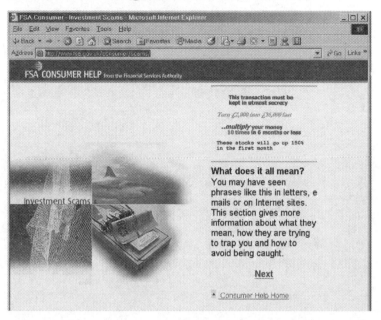

When the Internet came into being, so did a whole range of new scams. There are a number of web sites that deal with scams, but this is one of the best. It is actually part of the FSA site. It covers various types of scam, and not just the Internet variety. There are several sections with each one devoted to a different type of fraud. First you are shown the approach by the fraudsters, then the details of the fraud, and finally there is advice on how to avoid getting caught. There is also a useful section that provides links to other sites that provide information about scams and avoiding them. If you are new to the Internet and using Email it is well worthwhile going through the information on this site and some of the linked sites.

5　Financial sites

The Motley Fool (www.fool.co.uk)

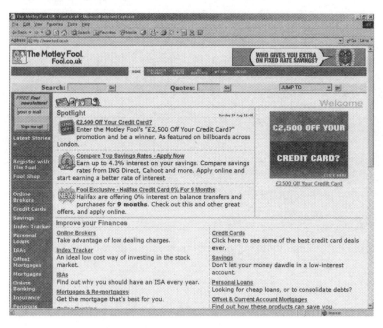

The Motley Fool is an American company that has branched out into the UK. It publishes numerous books on all matters financial. Although it is best known for its books on investment, the site also covers other topics such as credit cards and insurance. As the name of the company and the site address suggest, things are treated in a light-hearted manner in an attempt to make mortgages and insurance fun. The advice given is accurate and sound though. It is a large site that provides articles on various aspects of finance, plus stock market data and quotes, a discussion board, and much more.

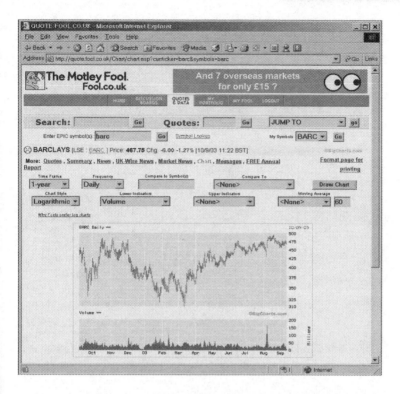

If you would like to learn more about financial matters you will probably find plenty of interest on this site. Much of the site's content is aimed at beginners, but there is also some material for those with some experience of the financial world. Of course, you can buy Motley Fool books online from this site. One slight weakness of this site is the small pop-up advertisements that appear each time you move to a new page. It is necessary to go through a registration process in order to access most of the content, but registration is free.

5   Financial sites

Amp (www.iii.co.uk)

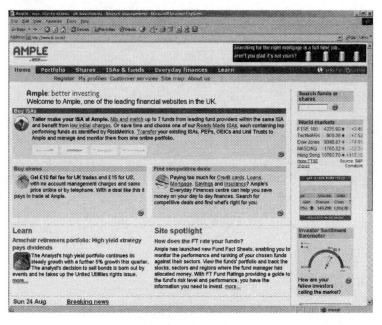

This site was originally called International Interactive Investor, but it was bought a few years ago by the Amp, the large Australian company. Many of the original features were retained though, so it is more than just a site to promote the products of Amp. The original site covered investing rather than general financial matters, and there is still a bias towards investment. However, there is some general financial coverage of topics such as travel insurance, mortgages, and credit cards in the Everyday Finances section.

TrustNet (www.trustnet.com)

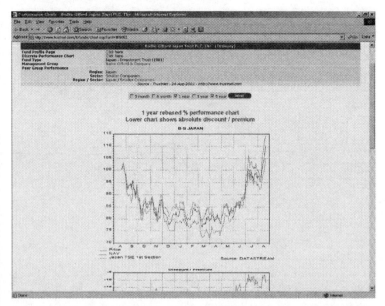

TrustNet is quite definitely not a general financial site. It specialises in investment funds such as unit trusts and investment trusts. A number of educational guides are available from this site, so it is worth looking at these if you do not know your ISA from your ETF. The main purpose of the site is to provide data on funds such as unit trusts, investment trusts, and venture capital trusts. You can look up the current unit or share price for practically any UK based fund. There are contact details for the manager of each fund including (where applicable) a link to their web site. There is also data showing the past performance of each fund and you can even draw graphs showing the historic performance of a fund. A great site for performance monitoring or selecting funds.

Fund advice

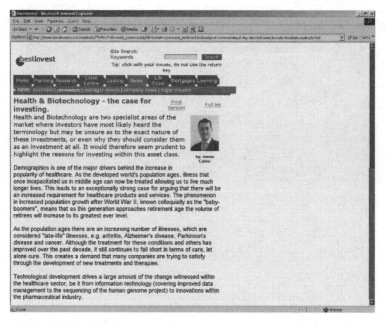

Several of the larger independent financial advisors have web sites that provide news and information about investing. The type of content varies significantly from one site to another, but there are often articles about specific types of investment, news on changes in fund management, and this type of thing. These four sites are worthy of investigation:

www.bestinvest.com

www.chartwell-investment.co.uk

www.h-l.co.uk (Hargreaves-Lansdown)

www.allenbridge.co.uk

Education (www.schwab-europe.com)

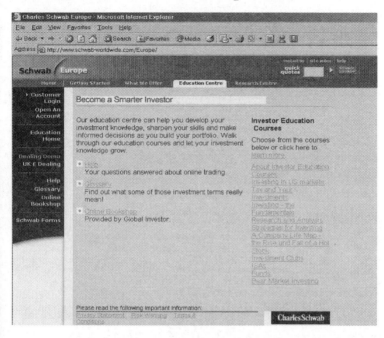

Charles Schwab is a stockbroker and the European arm of the company is now owned by Barclays. Their web site includes what they call an Education Centre where you can learn about various financial topics. All of the courses are free. The information on the sites of other brokers tends to be much less wide ranging, but useful background information about share dealing can be found on these sites:

www.halifax.co.uk

www.tdwaterhouse.co.uk

www.stocktrade.co.uk

5 Financial sites

DigitalLook (www.digitallook.com)

There are plenty of sites offering financial news. DigitalLook provides research on individual companies, news about market activity, directors' dealings, etc. There are also sections that deal with funds and personal finance. The personal finance section includes guides to online banking, home insurance, credit cards. It is therefore more than just a financial news site. Much of the content seems to be accessible without registering with the site. You do have to register in order to use some of the more advanced features, but registration is free. It is a site that is actually much bigger than it appears to be at first, so take some time to explore it.

ShareCast (www.sharecast.com)

ShareCast is now effectively part of the DigitalLook site, and it can be accessed via a link on the DigitalLook site. It remains a separate site though, and it can be accessed directly at the address provided here. Unlike DigitalLook, this site is exclusively about financial news and reports. In addition to the news stories on the site there is a roundup of the financial news in the press. About the only non-news facility I have found is a facility for charting stocks. This is one of the smaller financial web sites, but it is delightfully straightforward to use. CityWire (www.citywire.co.uk) is another financial news site that is worth a look, but some of its content is only available on subscription.

5   Financial sites

BBC News (www.bbc.co.uk/news)

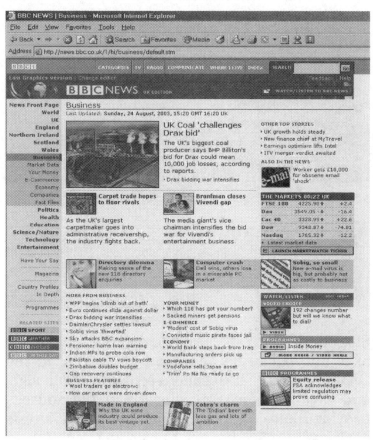

The BBC site seems to have just about everything, and it certainly has a very large news section. Left-click the Business link on the homepage of the news section and the business news page will appear. The "Business" link in the left-hand section of the page will expand to provide a menu that gives access to further pages of business and financial news.

Teletext (www.teletext.com/finance)

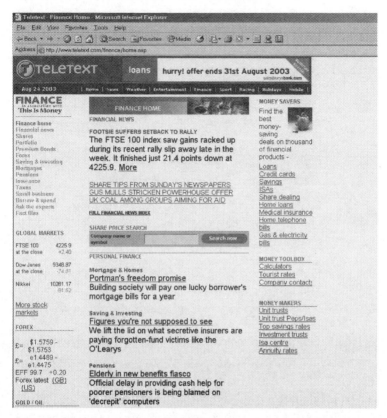

Teletext is available online, and as one would expect there is a financial news section. In fact the news section includes more than news, and there are articles on various aspects of personal finance and investing. Some of the content is actually provided by This Is Money (www.thisismoney.com), and is also available by going direct to this site.

Yahoo! (http://uk.finance.yahoo.com)

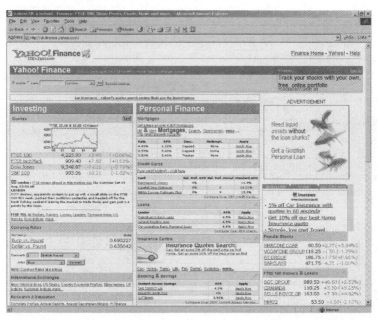

Yahoo! seems to provide a massive amount of financial news and data on all their web sites, and the UK site is certainly no exception. Stock quotes are available for the UK and more than a dozen other countries. These are delayed by about 20 minutes incidentally, and are not in real-time. Historic data is available and this can be downloaded to a spreadsheet program. A stock charting facility is available, each day there is a roundup of share tips from the newspapers, and there are beginners guides to insurance, mortgages, etc. You might also like to try Lycos (http://finance.lycos.com) and MSN (http://moneycentral.msn.com), but these are primarily aimed at users in the USA.

Reuters (www.reuters.co.uk)

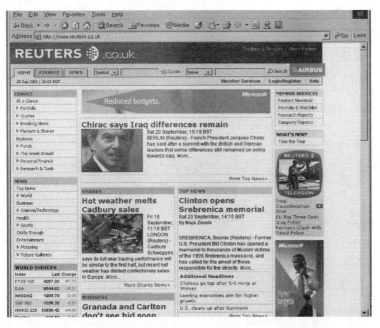

A lot of the financial news stories on the Internet originate from the Reuters news agency. Yahoo! for example, uses Reuters as its primary source for financial news and data. It is possible to "cut out the middle man" and go direct to the Reuters UK web site. This gives general news coverage, and the financial news can be accessed by operating the "Business" link on the homepage. The menu in the top left-hand section of the page provides access to stock quotes, charts, broker's forecasts, etc. The US version of the site is available at:

www.reuters.com

This has recorded television news reports.

ADVFN (www.advfn.com)

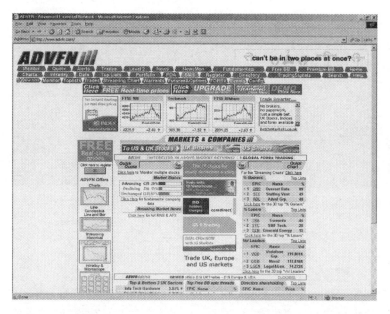

There is a certain amount of material for beginners on the ADVFN site, but it is primarily for experienced users who trade shares, covered warrants, etc. There is no information on such things as credit cards, personal loans, and insurance. You need to register with the site in order to get at most of the content, and the more advanced features are only available on subscription. ADVFN is one of the few sites to provide free real-time prices for UK shares. The free content also includes a large and popular bulletin board where you can discuss financial matters with other users. News is available from the site, and there is a free Email service where market reports are sent out three times per trading day. This is a great site for those who are deeply into stocks and shares.

MoneyAM (www.moneyam.com)

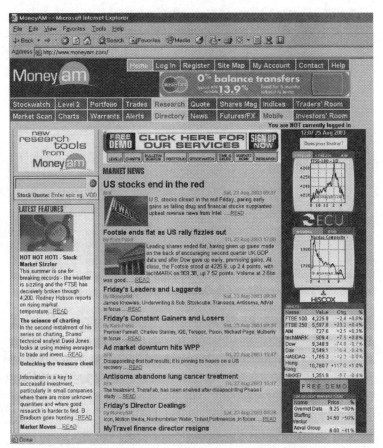

This is a relatively new site that was set up in direct competition to ADVFN. The facilities on offer are not identical to those of ADVFN but they are broadly similar. Like ADVFN, the more advanced features are only available on subscription.

UK-Analyst (www.uk-analyst.com)

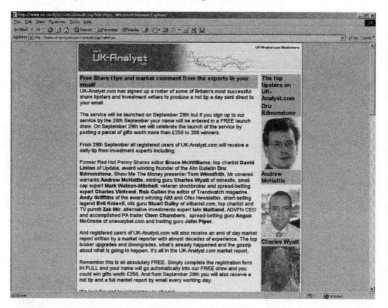

This site is so new that at the time of writing it has
not commenced operating in earnest. It should have
been in operation for a while by the time this book is
published. The idea is for each of 20 experts in various
aspects of finance to provide one article per month.
A new article will therefore be added to the site each
weekday. The articles will provide share tips, market
analysis, and general comment on the markets. It is
necessary to register with the site in order to access
the content, but registration is free. There has been
a general trend on the Internet for the type of thing
that was once free to be available only on subscription.
This site seems to be trying to reverse that trend.
Presumably the contributors will be using this site to
promote their own sites and publications.

Inland Revenue (www.inlandrevenue.gov.uk)

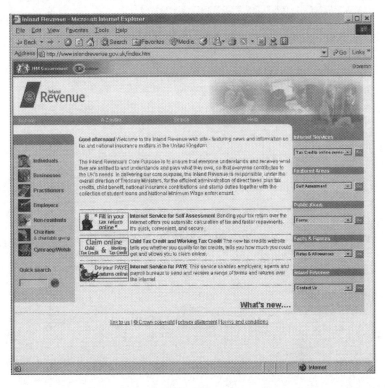

There are plenty of sites that give advice about income tax and other types of personal taxation, but this is the place to go if you require information "from the horse's mouth". There are various help and FAQ (frequently asked questions) sections and tax forms that can be downloaded. These days you can even fill in your self-assessment forms online and get your tax bill calculated in an instant. Fortunately, this site is easier to navigate than the average tax form.

Money Supermarket
(www.moneysupermarket.com)

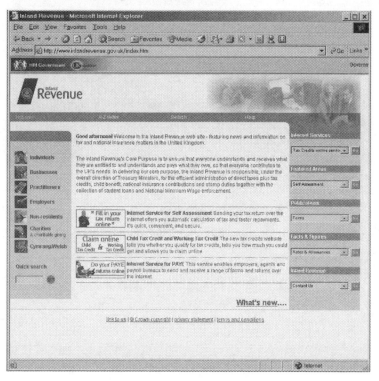

There are several sites that provide comparisons of financial products so that you can find the best deals. Money Supermarket is probably the biggest UK site of this type, and amongst others it provides comparisons of credit cards, loans, and motor insurance. Of course, there is little to be gained if you already have good deals, but many people save hundreds of pounds a year simply by switching to different bank accounts, etc.

Which? (www.switchwithwhich.co.uk)

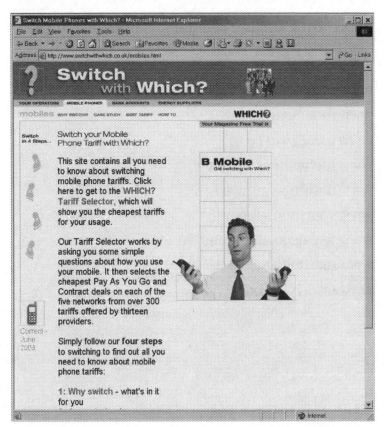

This site is run by the publishers of the well known Which? magazine. The site, like the magazine, takes no advertising and therefore has some justification in claiming to be completely impartial. The aim of the site is much the same as that of the Money Supermarket site. It tries to find you a better deal for mobile phone tariffs, current accounts, tour operators, and energy suppliers.

Not only but also

There are a number of other good financial sites, and these are all worth a look:

www.bloomberg.co.uk

www.moneyxtra.com

www.trade2win.co.uk

www.tacticaltrader.com

www.nothing-ventured.com

www.yourmoney.com

www.tiscali.co.uk/money

www.uswitch.com

www.unravelit.com

Heath and fitness

Self help

For as long as medical encyclopaedias have been available it has been possible to read through one and find that you have the symptoms of just about every disease known to man. It would be easy to fall into the same trap by going to some of the health and fitness sites on the Internet. There is a vast amount of useful information out there on these subjects, but this information must be used sensibly. Do not let your imagination run wild. If it is clear that you need medical attention, the place to go is your doctor and not a web site. On the fitness side of things, try not to get carried away. A fitness regime designed for an Olympic athlete is not going to be suitable for you or me! If you suffer from a serious medical condition it is essential to consult your doctor before starting on any form of exercise.

An important point to bear in mind is that there are plenty of web sites offering cures for just about anything, but they are mostly scams of one sort or another. Using these sites you could soon lose lots of money, damage your health, and perhaps import an illegal substance. Stick to the respectable sites and give the rest "a wide berth".

6   Health and fitness

ASH (www.ash.org.uk)

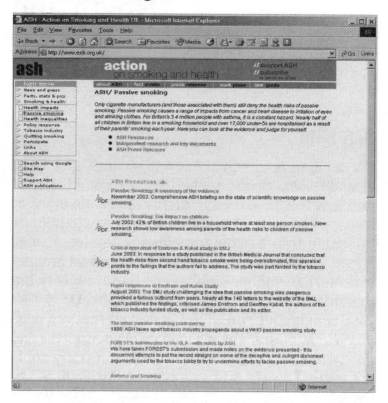

A large percentage of doctors seem to agree on the
best way to improve the health and fitness of the
nation, and that is for everyone to quit smoking. ASH
(Action on Smoking and Health) is the biggest
organisation in the UK that campaigns on this issue.
Their web site has a large amount of information on
smoking and passive smoking. As one would expect,
it does not "pull its punches". There is, of course, a
large section devoted to giving up smoking.

BBC (www.bbc.co.uk/health)

Yet another useful section of the BBC's "mega" web site. Its primary purpose is to support the BBC television and radio programs that deal with health and fitness, but there are numerous articles about health matters. There is in fact a subsection that deals with health and fitness at 50+, and there are plenty more articles in other parts of the site that cover topics of interest to this age group.

NHS Direct (www.nhsdirect.nhs.uk)
NHS Direct Wales (www.nhsdirect.wales.nhs.uk)

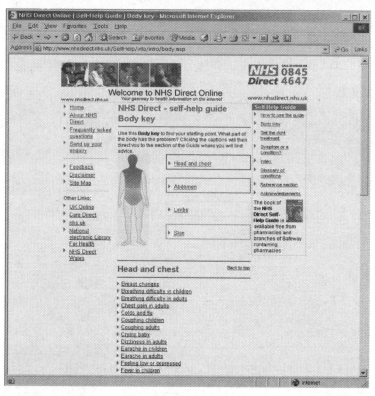

This is a government web site that is designed to prevent the National Health Service from being clogged up by minor ailments and hypochondriacs. It is the online version of the well-known telephone helpline service. There is information about a wide range of illnesses, and what I suppose is a sort of self-diagnosis system where you can find out the likely cause of your symptoms. It is a huge online resource that can be extremely useful if used sensibly.

Health Centre (www.healthcentre.org.uk)

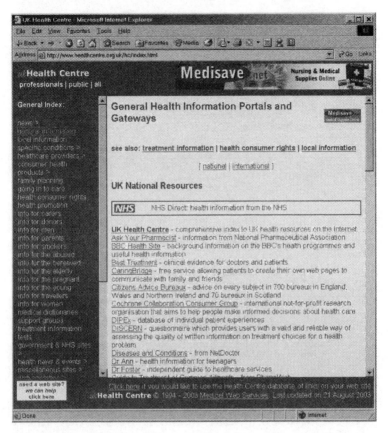

Apparently this site was set up by a GP in order to give patients access to good and reliable medical information via the Internet. The strength of the site is not so much in the medical information it contains, as in the huge number of links it provides. If you need to know about a particular disease for example, it will probably be possible to find a link to some information via this site.

Travelling (www.doh.gov.uk/traveladvice)

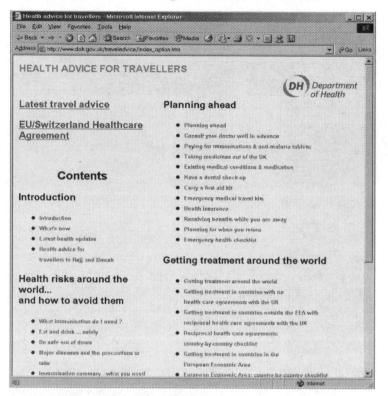

Travelling abroad and catching something nasty seems to be a growth industry. This site is maintained by the Department of Health, and its purpose is to provide information about staying healthy when travelling overseas. It also has sections that give advice on what to do if you should be injured or fall ill while outside the UK. Definitely worth a look, particularly if you are about to travel to somewhere exotic.

Cancer BACUP (www.bacup.org.uk)

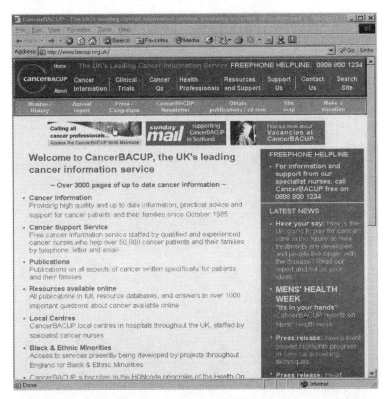

This site claims to be the UK's biggest cancer information service, and it is probably fully justified in making this claim. The site has detailed information about various types of the cancer and the treatments for each one. There are links to NHS online leaflets and a range of publications can be bought from this site. A great deal of information about coping with cancer is on offer, which is largely what this site is about.

Keep Fit (www.keepfit.org.uk)

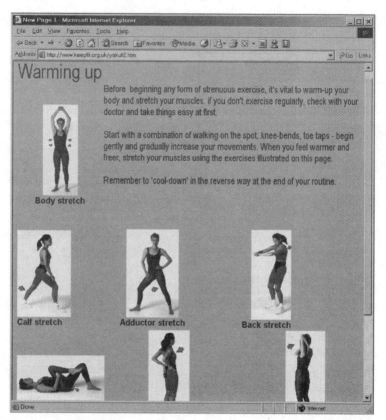

If you are reading this book you are presumably old enough to remember Eileen Fowler and her keep fit programs on the television. This method of exercise is still going strong, and it is promoted by The Keep Fit Association. Their site has details of some exercises that you can try for yourself, complete with plenty of illustrations. There are also details of joining the association and attending local classes.

Walking (www.whi.org.uk)

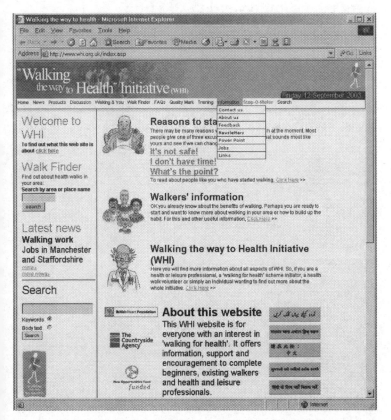

This is the site of the Walking for Health Initiative. It explains the benefits of walking in order to keep healthy and gives advice on such things as how far and fast to walk and how often. It is a much smaller and simpler site than most of the others featured here, but it tells you what you need to know in straightforward manner.

Age Concern (www.ageconcern.co.uk/AgeConcern/information_358.htm)

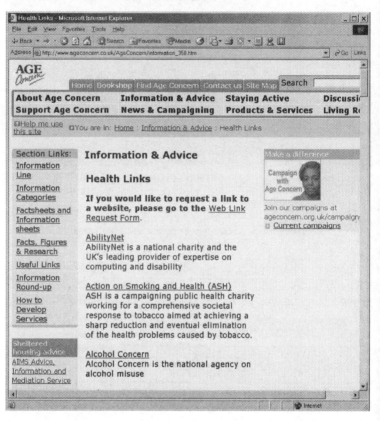

The Age Concern site is featured in chapter 3. This is a page of that site that provides links to a number of health related sites. There are links to sites dealing with specific illnesses such as Alzheimer's, sites dealing with disability and mobility problems, and sites covering the general area of health and fitness. There are links to numerous top quality health and fitness sites here.

Hobbies

Spare time

We supposedly have more leisure time as we get older, but I can not say that I have actually noticed this effect yet. Anyway, the Internet is the ideal for people wishing to tell the world about their hobbies, and for companies trying to sell hobby related goods. On the internet there are sites that cover pretty well everything from sky surfing (www.skysurfer.com) to bog snorkelling (http://llanwrtyd-wells.powys.org.uk/bog.html). Strangely, the ultimate in easy to remember (or should that be difficult to forget?) Internet addresses, www.bogsnorkelling.com, is still "up for grabs".

There are certainly too many hobbies and pastimes to cover them all here, but a range of hobbies that are popular with the "Saga" generation will be considered. Using a good search engine such as Google it should not be difficult to find sites for the more unusual hobbies. The size and quality of the sites for minority interests varies enormously, but there are some good ones out there if you are prepared to spend some time looking for them. There are several good and large sites for most of the more popular hobbies.

Local clubs (www.uk-websitesdirectory.co.uk)

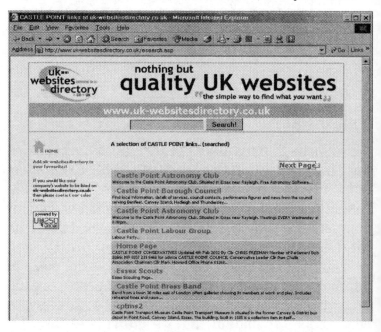

It is worth bearing in mind that there are local societies and clubs for many hobbies and sports. Also, local authorities run part time courses for many creative hobbies (painting, flower arranging, etc.), and in some cases a few sports as well. Most local councils now have a web site, and this should give details of the available courses or tell you how to obtain details. This site is actually a general search engine for web sites in the UK. However, if you use the name of your town, local authority area, or nearby towns as search strings, it will usually produce many links for local clubs and societies. It should also provide the Internet address for your local authority and nearby local authorities.

Boating (www.ybw.com)

This is the companion site for Yachting and Boating World magazine, and the menu near the top left-hand corner provides easy access to a range of boating related magazine sites. Obviously the sites are designed to promote the magazines, but they contain a lot of boating news, forums where users of the sites can discuss boating matters, a directory of boating related businesses, and much else. Definitely the best feature is the massive database of new and used boats that are for sale. If you are not in the market for a boat it is good fun to "window shop" for your ideal yacht.

Walking (www.ramblers.org.uk)

This is the site of The Ramblers' Association, which is the main organisation for those who like to go for country walks. If you wish to find details of group walks in a particular area or details of your local rambling groups, with the aid of this site you should quickly and easily find what you are looking for. There are also news stories, information on getting started, and much else in this huge and impressive site.

Lawn bowls (www.lawnbowls.com.au)

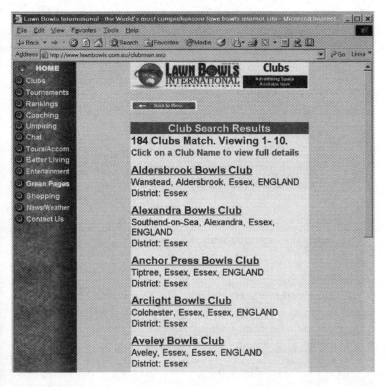

Realistically, one would not expect bowls to have the same sort of presence on the Internet as (say) football, which is just as well because there are surprisingly few sites devoted to this sport. There are some good sites, but some of them are spoilt by the barrage of pop-ups that appear when you enter the site or change pages. This site seems to be free from pop-ups, and although it is based in Australia it provides worldwide coverage. The directory of clubs includes the UK, and just about everywhere else. There are news and results for the major tournaments around the world.

Golf (www.golftoday.co.uk)

I can not claim to be a golf fan, but this site seems to be highly rated by many of those that are. It carries a large number of reports on tournaments and other golf related stories. The coverage concentrates on Europe, but there is also some worldwide coverage. There is a directory of UK golf courses with contact information and some basic details for each one.

SAA (www.saa.co.uk)

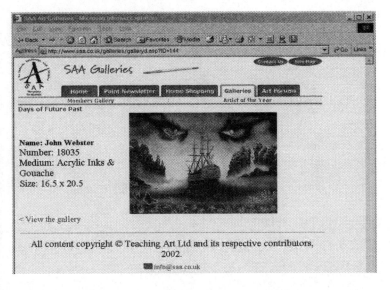

As far as I am aware there is only one national organisation in the UK for amateur artists, and this is the Society for Amateur Artists (SAA). There is a commercial aspect to this organisation and site, but the commercial interests are not allowed to dominate things. It does mean that a lot of the material on the site is from top professionals in the art teaching world. You do not have to be a member of the SAA in order to access their site, but you do have to join the national organisation in order to join one of the local groups. It is a relatively new organisation that was set up in 1992, so there are likely to be older art societies in your area as well as the SAA groups. The site contains galleries of members' pictures and tutorials by experts. It is well worth a look if you are an amateur artist or would like to become one.

Gardening (www.bbc.co.uk/gardening)

Apparently a recent study concluded that elderly gardeners are fitter than the average teenager. Gardening is traditionally the main pastime of the retired, so one might expect there to be numerous large sites devoted to gardening in retirement. I have not managed to find even one, but most general sites for the retired have a section dealing with gardening. Also, most general gardening sites seem to assume that most of their visitors will be at least middle-aged, and slant their coverage accordingly. The BBC site has a section on gardening that matches their extensive television coverage of this subject. There are numerous articles giving advice for beginners and more experienced gardeners. You can even listen to a recording of the most recent Gardeners Question Time radio program.

Gardening (www.rhs.org.uk)

This is the web site of the RHS (Royal Horticultural Society), and as one would expect it contains news, advice, and information about the RHS itself. Visiting gardens is a pastime that has become phenomenally popular in recent years. There is a useful garden finding facility that enables gardens in a particular area that meet certain criteria to be listed. In a similar vein there is a gardening event finder and there is also a plant finder. The letter enables you to find sources for rare and exotic plants, or the more mundane ones.

Gardening (www.thegardener.btinternet.co.uk)

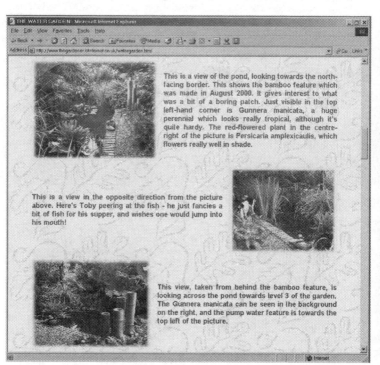

There are many gardening sites run by enthusiasts, and many of these are very good. This one is the brainchild of Chris Harten, and it is one of the biggest as well as being one of the best. It is produced more professionally than many a professional web site. Definitely worth a look if you are interested in gardening, or web design come to that.

Flower arranging
(www.thegardener.btinternet.co.uk/tips.html)

The Internet seems to be the ideal place to show off beautiful flower arrangements, but good flower arranging sites seem to be few and far between. This one is excellent, and is actually part of the gardening site mentioned in the previous section. Remember that most local authorities run part-time courses on flower arranging, but they will probably be called "floral art" or "floral design" courses.

Food (www.bbc.co.uk/food)

Cooking programs are another mainstay of the BBC's television output, and there are food related radio programs as well. It is therefore no surprise that the BBC's web site has a large section dealing with this subject. Some of the content is to promote or support television programs, but there is much else besides. In particular, there is a huge range of recipes and a search engine to help you track down the right ones. I tried searching for "Peking duck" and "bread butter pudding", and there were several matches for each one. Virtually every recipe from every BBC cooking program seems to be included on the site!

Food (http://recipes.sainsburys.co.uk)

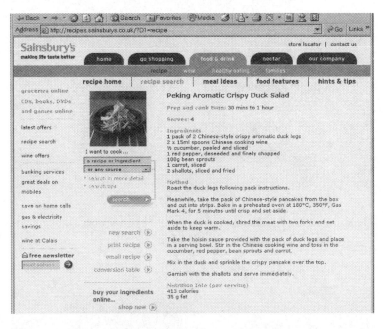

This is part of the site for J Sainsbury, the big supermarket chain. If you live in the right part of the country you can order online and they will deliver your groceries, as will others including Tesco and Iceland. The sites of the big supermarkets often have a few recipes to encourage you to buy their food products, and these recipes are presumably all tried, tested and of good quality. The Sainsbury's site has a huge range of recipes together with general information on handling, storing, and cooking foods. If the BBC and Sainsbury sites do not provide what you are looking for, typing the name of a dish or its main ingredients into a search engine, plus the word "recipe", will probably produce the recipe you are after.

Photography (www.nyip.com)

The New York Institute of Photography has been providing correspondence courses on photography for as long as I can remember. Actually, it was founded in 1910, so I suppose it has been doing its correspondence courses for a lot longer than I can remember. It is an American organisation, but it operates worldwide. You do not have to be one of their customers to use most of this site. A number of interesting articles can be found in the "Photo Tips of the Month" section.

Digital photography (www.dpreview.com)

There are a number of sites that provide reviews of the latest digital cameras and related equipment, but this site has the advantage of looking at things from a UK perspective. There are several good American digital photography sites, but some of the cameras are sold under different names in the UK, and in a few cases might not be sold here at all. These US sites are well worth a look:

www.dcresource.com

www.steves-digicams.com

www.imaging-resource.com

Crosswords (www.crosswordsite.com)

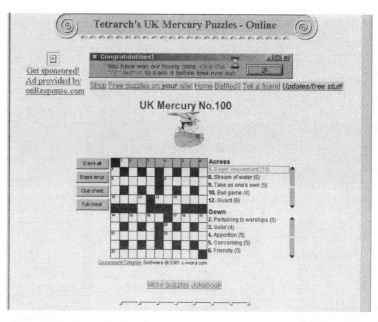

Many retired persons use crosswords and other puzzles to keep their minds active. At one time there were daily crosswords available free of charge from newspaper sites, but many of these services have ceased or are only available on subscription. This site gives the option of US or UK crosswords, and the puzzles are available in three levels of difficulty plus a cryptic type. They can be solved onscreen or a printer-friendly version can be selected. The crosswords can be printed in the same manner as any web pages. Select the Print option from the File menu or right-click on the page and select Print from the pop-up menu. As far as I can see there is no charge for using this site.

Games (http://uk.games.yahoo.com)

There have been computer games for almost as long as there have been computers. Although the term "computer games" tends to conjure up images of all-action games with racing cars or fighter planes, there are many other types of computer game. These include card games, mah-jong, chess, backgammon, and draughts. This site it part of Yahoo! UK, and it enables you to play solitaire games, compete with others online, and download demonstration versions of commercial games. The latter are always limited in some way, such as only functioning for a few days, but can be fun. Note that you have to register with Yahoo! in order to use the facilities of this site. The UK arm of MSN offer similar facilities at this address:

http://uk.zone.msn.com

DIY (www.diy.com)

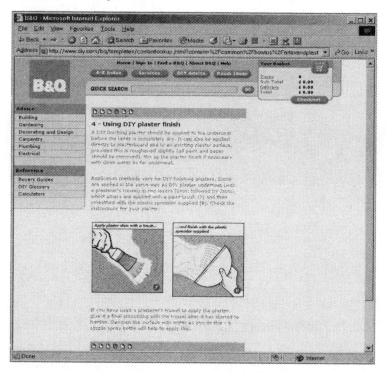

These days DIY is very big business, and it has quite a large presence on the Internet. This site is actually the online version of a B&Q store, and it can be used to buy a wide range of DIY products online. However, it is more than just an online store, and operating the "DIY Advice" button at the top of the page takes you into a large section that provides help on a wide range of DIY topics. It is effectively an online DIY encyclopaedia, and it provides useful information about decorating, repairs, flooring, and just about any DIY project.

DIY (www.ukdiyguide.co.uk)

This site is directory and search engine for DIY sites. It provides links to suppliers, sites that provide advice, and even sites for DIY related television programs such as Changing Rooms. The latter is one that you have to see to believe, and it is at:

www.bbc.co.uk/homes/changingrooms

Fishing (www.fishing.co.uk)

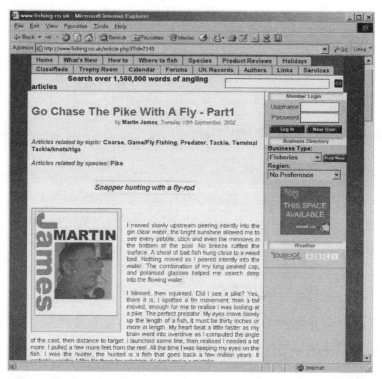

It is disapproved of by many, but it is supposedly Britain's favourite pastime. I suspect it is actually the second favourite, but it is certainly very popular in this country. Any good search engine will soon locate nearly a million fishing related sites, so you will need to be more specific in order to keep the number of matches within reason. Alternatively you can try this site, which is huge. It might not cover the type of fishing that you wish to learn about, but it seems to have articles and other information on most types of fishing.

Crafts directory
(http://uk.dir.yahoo.com/arts/Crafts)

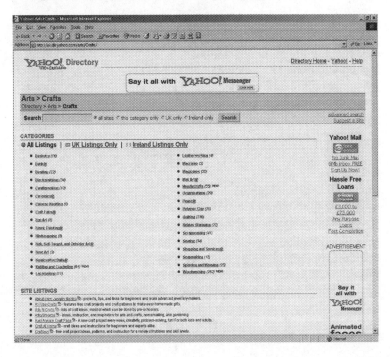

If you wish to find craft sites it is worth visiting this section of the Yahoo! directory. It lists a number of crafts, and operating one of the links takes you into a list of sites for that particular craft. In this example I operated the "Knitting and Crocheting" link, and it produced a large list of related sites. Many of these have links to other sites, and one such example is shown here. If a directory has a section that matches your area of interest it will usually produce more

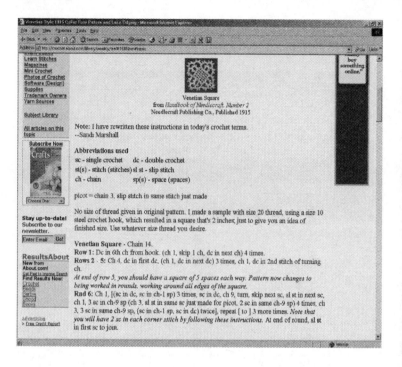

focussed and useful results than a search engine. A number of sections in the Yahoo! directory are concerned with pastimes such as art, crafts, boats, cars, and so on. There is actually a hobbies section at this address:

http://uk.dir.yahoo.com/Recreation/Hobbies

Antiques (www.bbc.co.uk/antiques)

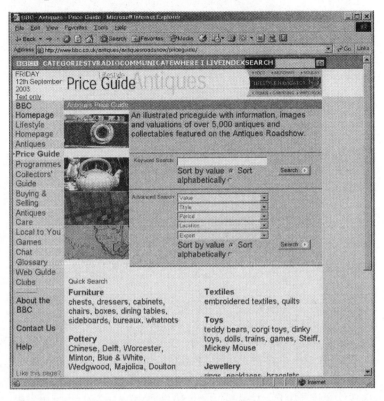

There are a large number of sites about antiques and collectables, but most of them are trying to sell you something rather than educate. This site is an exception. The enormous popularity of the BBC's shows relating to collecting and antiques have resulted in a substantial section devoted to these on their web site. With a subject as vast as this there is no single site that will tell you about every type of antique of collectable, but the BBC's site will keep enthusiasts busy for quite a while.

Auctions (www.ebay.co.uk)

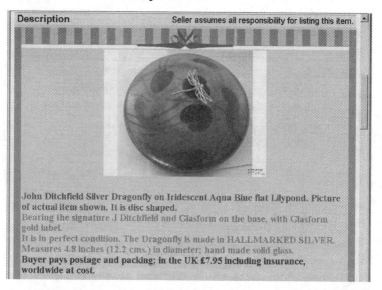

Description   Seller assumes all responsibility for listing this item.

John Ditchfield Silver Dragonfly on Iridescent Aqua Blue flat Lilypond. Picture of actual item shown. It is disc shaped.
Bearing the signature J Ditchfield and Glasform on the base, with Glasform gold label.
It is in perfect condition. The Dragonfly is made in HALLMARKED SILVER. Measures 4.8 inches (12.2 cms.) in diameter; hand made solid glass.
Buyer pays postage and packing; in the UK £7.95 including insurance, worldwide at cost.

The Internet has revolutionised the buying and selling of all sorts of things, but its impact in the collectables world has probably been the biggest. Many conventional auction houses now have a presence on the Internet, but there are also purely Internet auctions. By far the largest Internet auction company is Ebay, which is an American company that also operates in the UK and many other countries. You have to register with Ebay (and most other online auction companies) in order to buy or sell goods, but the registration process is fairly simple. There is plenty of online information to explain how things work. Just about everything turns up on Ebay eventually. One chap sold his soul, but I seem to remember that he only received about 20 dollars. Presumably the postage and packing was extra!

Travel

Grand tour

Some are predicting that in due course no one will bother to go and see the grand sites of the world. Instead you will just don your virtual reality headset and go online to visit The Grand Canyon, Ayers Rock, or wherever. There are certainly web cams that let you see all sorts of places on the Internet, and a few virtual tours, but we are still a long way from the full virtual reality experience.

The web is closely associated with travel. You can book holidays, flights, and theatre tickets online, but there is also a huge amount of travel information, maps, and details of virtually any destination. Many hotels have online video tours or photo albums so that you can see the interior and the grounds before you book. Another common facility is a panning 360 degree view of the interior or exterior of the hotel. The image shown here is from a panning view outside the Tower Thistle hotel in London. The Internet is not just a convenient way of booking holidays. It can help you to get to your destination and it will show exactly what you will find when you get there.

Thistle Tower External View

UK maps (http://uk.maps.yahoo.com)

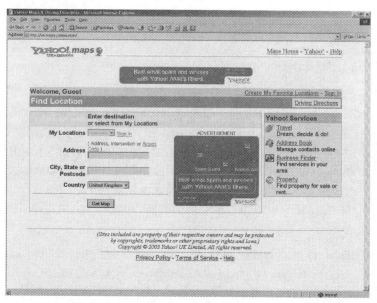

Many journeys seem to consist of about two hours driving to the right area, half an hour driving around trying to find exactly the right place, and three days trying to park. The Internet will not park your car for you, but it can help you to quickly locate the correct address. This is part of the UK Yahoo! site, and it will provide a local map for just about anywhere in the UK. My previous attempts to find a photograph of Neasden High Street were unsuccessful, but using this facility immediately produced a map of the area. You simply have to provide a basic address plus postcode and it then produces a map showing that area of the country. The Map Navigation panel to the right of the map enables the level of zoom to be varied, so you can zoom in for a more detailed view. The star-

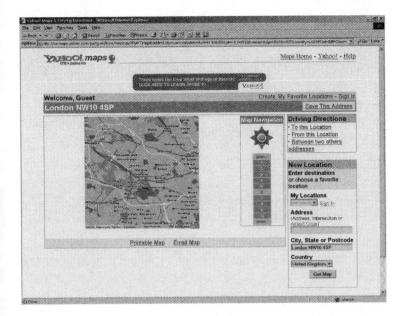

shaped icon is actually a control that enables the map
to be panned in the desired direction. If you would
like a printed map to take with you on the journey,
operate the "Printable Map" link. Then in the new
page, operate the "click here" link to go ahead and
print the map via your printer.

It is possible to get directions from one location to
another by activating the "To This Location" link near
the top right-hand corner of the page. This produces
a new page where the starting address is added, and
the destination address is edited if you wish to change
to a new one. Operating the "Get Directions" button
produces a map showing the route, a more detailed
map of the destination area, and a list of instructions.
This is definitely one of the best free services on the
Internet.

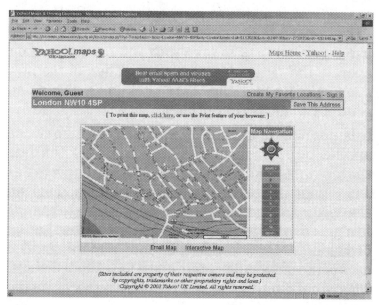

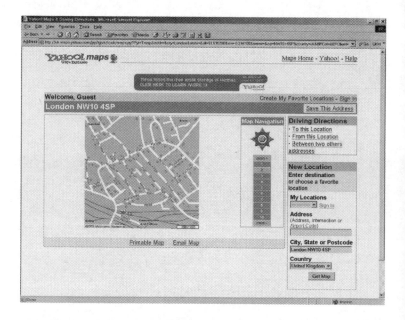

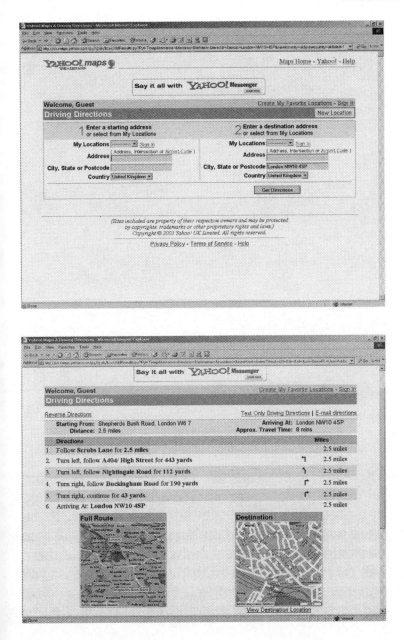

More maps (www.multimap.com)

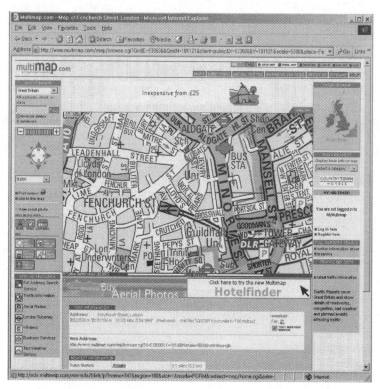

There are other map sites, and this is one of the more interesting ones. You provide it with a street name or a postcode and operate the "Find" button. If you use a postcode a map of the appropriate area will then be produced. With street names it is likely that there will be several streets with the same name, so you will then be supplied with a list so that you can select the correct one. The appropriate map will then be

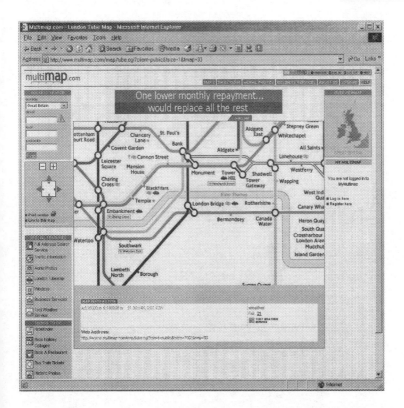

produced. It is possible to pan and zoom the map using the controls on to the left of the map. You can get a low definition aerial photograph of an area by operating the "aerial Photos" button, and there is a facility that enables a higher quality photograph to be purchased. There is also a facility that produces an onscreen map of the London Underground system.

And more maps (www.maporama.com)

Maporama is another site that provides street maps, and it seems to cover most of Europe and some other countries. You just supply the name of a town and (optionally) a postcode, and it will produce a map of the area. As with the other map sites, there are controls that permit panning and zooming. This site also has a route finder, and this again requires a town and optional postcode, but for both start and finish locations. A map showing the route is then produced, together with an impressively detailed list of instructions.

Yet more maps (http://mappoint.msn.co.uk)

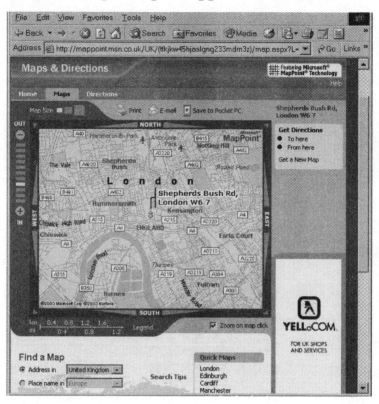

Mappoint is one of Microsoft's sites, and it can provide maps for the UK and elsewhere in Europe. As usual, you supply a basic address and the site responds with a map of the area. Maps for several large UK cities are available via the links on the homepage. There is also a route planner facility where you can opt for the quickest or shortest route. This is another route planner that provides an impressively detailed list of directions. It correctly negotiates the one-way system in my area.

Trains (www.nationalrail.co.uk)

Browser window showing:

Train Times for London Fenchurch Street

- For more information contact National Rail Enquiries on 08457 48 49 50.
- London Fenchurch Street station is managed by Network Rail.
- These train times are produced by an automated system. Our disclaimer explains its limitations.
- This page updates every 2 minutes. Click here for a version that does not automatically update.

Last updated: 01/09/2003 20:23:02

From	Timetabled Arrival	Expected Arrival	To	Timetabled Departure	Expected Departure	Operator
Shoeburyness	2022	2031	**Terminates**			c2c
Grays	2026	On time	**Terminates**			c2c
London Fenchurch Street			Shoeburyness	2030	No report	c2c
Southend Central	2035	On time	**Terminates**			c2c
London Fenchurch Street			Grays	2035	No report	c2c

The railways never seem to be out of the news, and they usually hit the headlines for all the wrong reasons. Nevertheless, they are used by millions every day and are still loved by many. This site is maintained by National Rail, which replaced the now defunct Railtrack PLC. The site is probably best known for its "live" departure boards, which are accessed appropriately enough, by the "Live Departure Boards" button on the homepage. Select

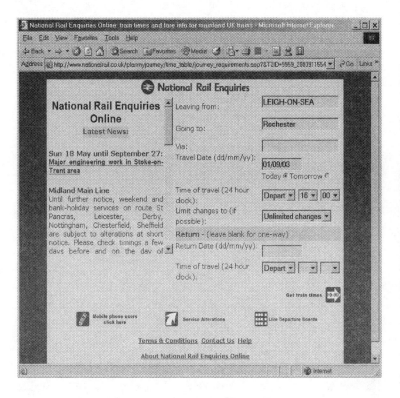

your station using the search engine on the new page that appears, and then the appropriate departure board will appear. The boards are generated automatically and updated every two minutes. There are a few caveats about their accuracy. Perhaps of more practical use, operating the "Planning Your Journey" button on the homepage produces a screen where the starting and destination stations are selected, together with an approximate starting time. Then the "Get train times" button is operated, which will produce a list of options. Each of these will get you from one station to the other using the specified start time. If none of the arrival times meets your requirements it is possible to try earlier and later trains.

Travel news (www.bbc.co.uk/travel)

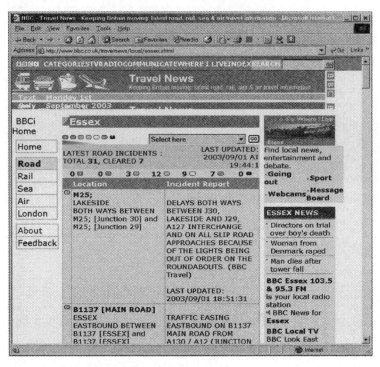

The BBC has a number of radio stations that seem to relish telling their listeners about the latest hold-ups on the roads, railways, ferries, or air routes. It therefore comes as no shock to learn that the BBC's web site has a large section that deals with travel matters. You select a mode of transport and an area of the country, and the site responds with a list of trouble spots. For this example I tried road travel in Essex, and surprise, surprise, there is a problem on the M25. I am not sure that I really needed the power of the Internet to tell me that. There are some useful links to other travel related sites.

Traffic news (www.theaa.com)

This is the site of the AA, and it includes a section that provides traffic news. You simply select an area and it shows the trouble spots on a map. Simply zoom in on an area using the onscreen controls and more detailed information about the problems will be provided. There are other useful facilities on this site including a good route planner for journeys within the UK.

UK guide (www.visitbritain.com)

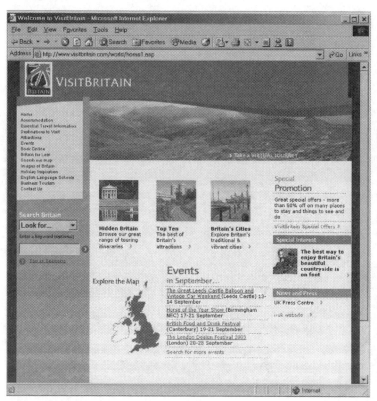

This rather anonymous looking site does not seem that impressive at first glance, but it is the official online tourist guide for Britain. There is a huge amount of information that can be accessed via the menus and the map. This includes details of accommodation for every area including camping sites, self catering, hotels, and B&Bs. There are also details of special events, places to visit, and masses of other information. Well worth a visit if you intend to explore Britain.

Rough Guides (www.roughguides.com)

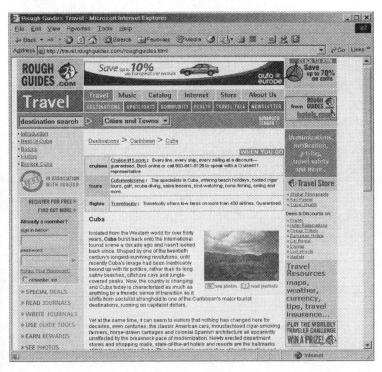

Left-click the "Destinations" link on the homepage and you will be taken to a list of guides for many parts of the world. The rough guides are known for telling it as it is. If a place is teaming with drug addicts, crooks, and prostitutes, and smells like a sewer, it will not be described as "having character". It will probably be described as "teaming with drug addicts, crooks, and prostitutes, and smells like a sewer". On the other hand, if a place is as good as the travel brochures suggest, it will say so. The other sections of the site are also worth exploring.

Beaches (www.seasideawards.org.uk)

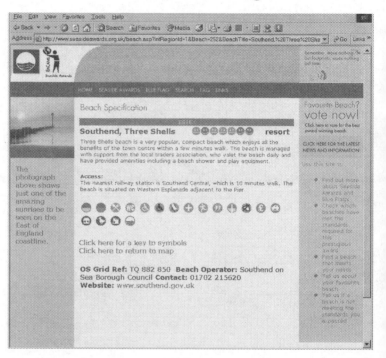

The cleanliness of beaches has been a hot topic in recent years, with some quite famous UK beaches failing to reach minimum EU standards. This site provides information about the standards reached (or failed) by hundreds of popular UK beaches. It also gives details of the facilities available at each beach via a simple system of icons. For example, you can check whether a given beach has access and toilet facilities for the disabled. In most cases there is a link to the web site of the local authority that controls each beach, where more detailed information is often available.

FOC (www.fco.gov.uk)

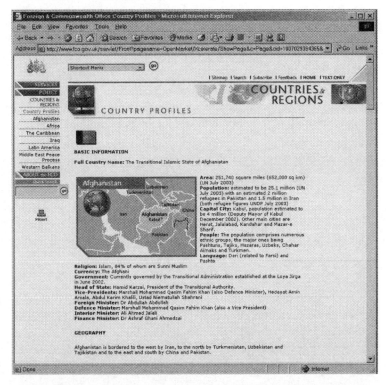

This is the web site of the Foreign and Commonwealth Office, and it contains a massive amount of information about travelling to overseas destinations. There is a section called "Know before you go", another one that gives information on what to do if things go wrong, and a large section that gives profiles of individual countries. There is plenty of down-to-earth advice here for anyone travelling abroad, but it is certainly a site that should be consulted before travelling to anywhere exotic. "Forewarned is forearmed" as the old adage says.

Farm Stay UK (www.farmstayuk.co.uk)

Staying on farms has been growing in popularity over a number of years. This is the web site of Farm Stay UK, which is the largest network of farm accommodation in the UK. The facilities of the site make it easy to find the required type of accommodation in any area of the UK. The accommodation is inspected in order to ensure that it achieves the required standard, so you should not find yourself sleeping in a hayloft.

News and weather

On demand

The Internet is well suited to supplying people with news, since pages can be rapidly updated. When you go onto a news site you should therefore find up-to-date news items. Unlike radio and television news, you do not have to tune in at certain times and wait to see if anything of interest turns up. You can go online at any time and quickly find the items that are of interest to you. It is rather like using the text facility of a television set, but it is generally faster to find what you require. Also, more in-depth coverage is usually available on the Internet.

The Internet is also well suited to weather forecasts. Pages can be updated regularly and there is no difficulty in using charts, maps, or even simple animations on Internet pages. If you are interested in how the weather is shaping up in the foreign resort you are about to visit, then there are probably several sites that will provide you with the answer. Not surprisingly perhaps, the number of sites that carry UK weather forecasts is huge.

BBC News (www.bbc.co.uk/news)

At the time of writing this, the BBC news service has itself been centre-stage in the news. Despite the controversy, the BBC news service remains one of the most respected in the business, and it is given due prominence on the BBC's web site. Incidentally, this is reputedly the biggest web site in Europe. The links on the BBC news homepage lead to pages devoted to the main areas of the UK and to various parts of the world. There are further links to special areas of interest such as technology and entertainment. In the list of links down the left-hand side of the page there is an "On This Day" link. This leads to a page that provides details of major news stories on the same day in earlier years.

Teletext (www.teletext.co.uk/news)

Teletext has been on the Internet for a number of years now, and it has a substantial web site that includes a large news section. Like the BBC news homepage, a list of links down the left-hand side of the page gives access to news for different regions and specialist areas of interest. There is also a very useful drop-down menu here that enables news for a specific area of the country to be selected. Teletext provides one of the most comprehensive online news services.

Reuters (www.reuters.co.uk)

Reuters is a name that is synonymous with news, so it is no surprise that this company has a large web site. Reuters is a "big player" in the world of financial news and data. This is probably the reason that business and financial news has its own list of links in the left-hand section of the homepage. However, there is a list of general news categories below this. This site's general news coverage seems to be less comprehensive than that provided by the BBC and Teletext sites. One slight drawback of the Reuters site is that there seems to be some very intrusive pop-up advertising, but this is the price you usually have to pay for free Internet services.

An interesting feature of this site is that it provides recorded television news reports that can be viewed by left-clicking the large television icon on the right-hand side of the homepage. This facility utilises Internet Explorer, the web browser that is normally installed as part of any Windows installation. It also requires either the Macromedia Flash Player or the Real One Player, so it might be necessary to download some software in order to make use of this feature. About half a dozen stories are available in each of five channels. The required channel is selected via the simple menu that is situated in the top left-hand corner of the player's window.

Guardian Unlimited (www.guardian.co.uk)

As one would probably expect, the UK newspapers have large presences on the Internet. There are a number of good news sites as a result. The Guardian Unlimited site is, as one would expect, the online version of the Guardian newspaper. It has a good range of stories but the site is not so vast that it is difficult to navigate. You can register with the site, but most of the content seems to be accessible without doing so. If you wish to refer back to an old story there is a searchable archive which should enable the required report to be located very quickly.

The Times (www.thetimes.co.uk)

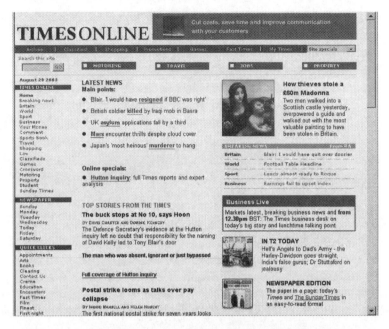

This is one of the larger of the sites associated with a newspaper, but it is reasonably easy to find the news items you require. In days of yore it was necessary to register with this site and logon in order to access its content, but there seems to be no current requirement to do this. Indeed, there no longer seems to be any facility to logon to the site. There is a searchable archive, and it is also possible to access online versions of the printed newspaper for the previous seven days. There seems to be free access to most of the site, but some of the content is only available on subscription. Unfortunately, these days the crosswords and puzzles are only available via a subscription service.

The Mirror (www.themirror.co.uk)

The tabloid newspapers are to be found on the Internet as well, and the online version of the Daily Mirror is straightforward and easy to use. It is perhaps on a smaller scale though, than some of the other newspaper sites. Unless I have missed something, the site's entire contents are free. There is the usual search facility that enables you to search for old stories and for pictures. The latter can be purchased online.

The Sun (www.thesun.co.uk)

The Sun newspaper is also online, and it is another
site that it is simple and straightforward to navigate.
Yes, there is an online version of page 3, complete
with a number of photographs of page 3 girls.

9   News and weather

Ananova (www.ananova.co.uk)

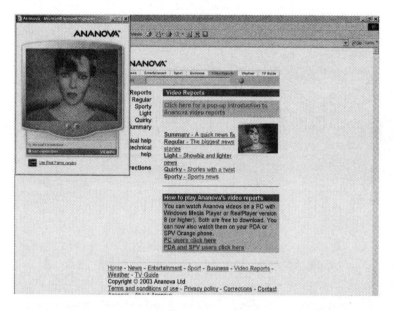

Ananova is one of the more interesting news sites. It has news in the usual categories, together with some quirky stories. There is also a good television guide that seems to cover all the stations available in the UK, including radio stations. The site's main claim to fame is that it has the world's first virtual news reader, appropriately called Ananova. Her recorded television news reports can be accessed via the "Video Reports" link on the homepage. Ananova is an animated character who "reads" the news via a speech synthesiser. Presumably the animation is also governed by the text that she "reads". There are a few odd results, but Ananova's rendition of the news is perfectly understandable. She will never replace Andrea Catherwood though!

UK Directory
(www.wrx.zen.co.uk/fromhere.htm)

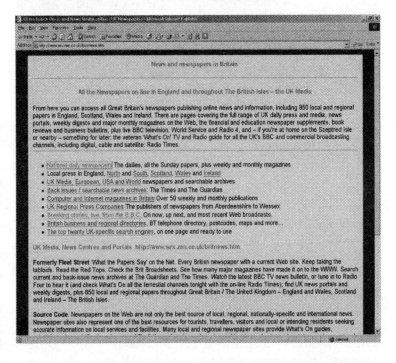

There are numerous online newspaper directories, and this one is useful for finding sites for UK newspapers. It includes the sites of local and provincial newspapers as well as the nationals. In fact there are links to many types of news-related sites located within the UK.

World Directory (www.nettizen.com/newspaper)

This directory includes links to a mind-boggling number of newspaper sites around the world. There are links to many UK local, regional and national newspapers. There are links to the Ferndown Times and the Tindle News for example. It provides similarly long lists for many other countries. There are links to the Cook Island News and the Illawarra Mercury for example. There are a few "dead" links, but this site seems to be reasonably up to date.

BBC Weather (www.bbc.co.uk/weather)

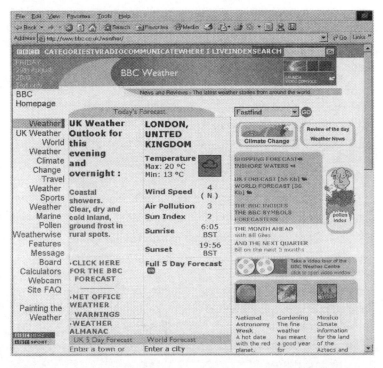

Virtually any site that has a news section will also have a section dealing with the weather, or will have a subsection of the news that deals with this subject. The BBC site has one of the Internet's largest collections of pages devoted to the weather. In addition to the UK weather forecast there are forecasts for most parts of the world, shipping forecasts, inshore forecasts, etc. There is also information on the pollen count, climate change, and other weather related subjects. The full five day forecast is very useful, but not guaranteed accurate of course.

9   News and weather

Met Office (www.metoffice.co.uk)

Many, but not all of the forecasts in the newspapers and on the television have their origins at the UK Meteorological Office (Met Office). You can get the forecasts "from the horse's mouth" by visiting their web site. Although one might expect the forecasts to be strictly for the UK, the site does in fact provide five day weather forecasts for most areas of the world. There is also background information about the Met Office.

Ananova Weather (www.ananova.co.uk/weather)

The Ananova site has an excellent section for UK weather. You can get the forecast for the nearest town to where you live, or the place you are about to visit. One slight disappointment is that the site that has the world's first virtual newsreader does not also have the world's first virtual weather girl. We will just have to make do with Sian Lloyd.

Small sites (www.xcweather.co.uk)

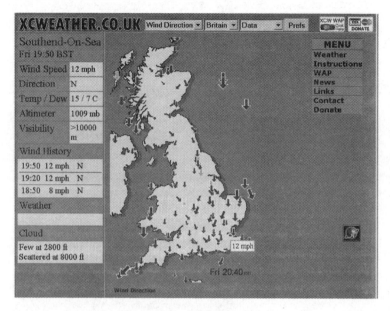

There are numerous small weather sites on the Internet, and some of them are quite interesting. This one has an interactive map of the UK. If you place the pointer over one of the places indicated on the map, the panel down the left-hand side of the page shows data for that place. Things such as wind speed and direction, temperature, and pressure are shown. It does not operate in real-time, but the readings normally seem to be no more than a few minutes old. It was interesting watching the temperatures in this area steadily escalate when the record for the highest temperature for the UK was broken. I live about 15 miles or so away from the record breaking town (Gravesend), so we only reached a little over 37 degrees Celsius!

BBC Sport (www.bbc.co.uk/sport)

The Internet is not exactly short of sites that carry sports news. Apart from the sites that carry general sports news there are official and unofficial sites for the various clubs, national teams, and sports stars. Using any good search engine it should not take long to find sites that deal with a specific club or sports person. The BBC's sports coverage may have reduced in scope over recent years, but the BBC web site has wide ranging coverage and remains one of the best. There are sections for the most popular sports plus more general sections. There is a lot of information about results, fixtures, and league tables.

9 News and weather

Ananova (www.ananova.co.uk/sport)

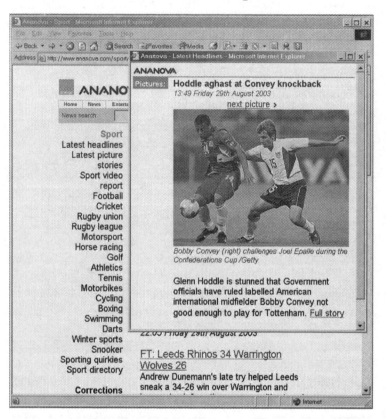

Ananova is another site that has a huge section dealing with sporting matters. Many sports have their own sections and there are some more general areas of the site. There is a picture story facility (a photograph plus a small amount of explanatory text), live scores, details of fixtures, league tables, and so on. Like the rest of the Ananova site, the sports section is comprehensive but easy to navigate.

Cricket (www.cricinfo.com)

As one would expect, there is a large number of sites devoted to cricket. Probably the best known is Cricinfo.com, which has a lot of information about domestic and international cricket. Unfortunately, many cricket sites only seem to cover test cricket. In addition to the coverage on the Cricinfo.com site there are numerous links to other cricket sites, including the official sites of the 18 county sides. These are also worth a look:

www.cricket4.com   www.cricnet.com

Football (www.footballunlimited.co.uk)

The Internet is supposedly dominated by porn sites, but the number of football sites probably runs porn a close second. This site is actually part of the Guardian Unlimited site, but it operates as what is effectively a separate site devoted to all things football. There is all the latest news about domestic, European club, and international football. Football often seems to be more about speculation than actually watching and playing the game, so the Rumour Mill section is essential reading. More mundanely, there is a section that provides the league tables. The All Talk section is a bulletin board where fans can discuss the latest hot topics in the football world.

Genealogy

Finding your roots

Genealogy is one of those pastimes that has achieved spectacular growth in recent years. The Internet has certainly helped to popularise genealogy, and has made it easier to research your family's past. However, many mistakenly believe that it will be possible to delve back into their family history using the Internet alone. In reality the Internet is a useful tool, but it usually has to be used in conjunction with the old fashioned methods. This means getting out and about to visit the places where your ancestors used to live.

If you do manage to trace your family history it is a good idea to pass on copies of your findings to other members of your family. An aunt of mine traced parts of the family tree back a few hundred years, and she told us about some of it. Unfortunately, when she died some years later her knowledge of the family's past died with her. This type of thing is not uncommon, so if you find anything interesting, share it with others in the family. They will probably be very willing to learn about their ancestors, especially if one of them is famous (or infamous).

A2A (www.a2a.pro.gov.uk)

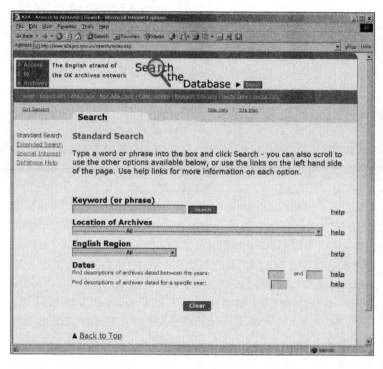

A2A (Access to Archives) is government site that catalogues 327 record offices in England and has 5.1 million catalogue entries dating back as far as 900. The archives are cared for in local record offices and libraries, universities, museums and national and specialist institutions across England. The data sources include deeds, hospital and police records, and business documents. As one would expect, the site has a search facility and there are various ways of sorting the search results. The archives at the record offices are all available to the public.

1901 Census (www.census.pro.gov.uk)

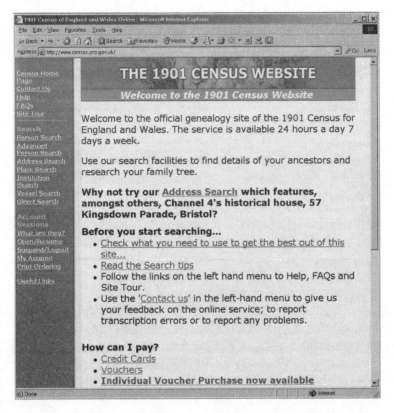

The contents of a census are largely secret for 100 years, so the 1901 census is the most recent one to be made available to all and sundry. This site was so popular when it was first launched that it became overloaded and was temporarily closed down. There is no charge for name and address searches, but it costs 50p for transcribed data for an individual, or 75p to view an image of a census page. Apparently there are records for over 32 million people.

Public Records Office (www.pro.gov.uk)

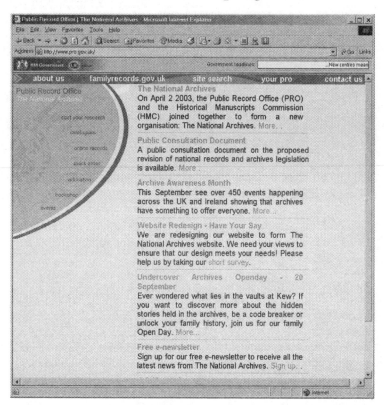

This is the main site of the Public Records Office. It is advisable to read the introduction which lists the records that are not catalogued on this site. Many types of record are covered here, but there are a number of exceptions. It has useful links to other government records sites.

Documents Online
(www.documentsonline.pro.gov.uk)

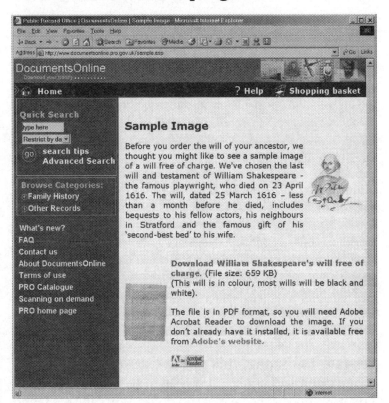

This is another site that is part of the Public Records Office, and it makes available many documents including over a million wills from the period 1384 to 1858. Searches and details of documents are free, but it costs £3 to download a document. However, Shakespeare's will is available as a free demonstration download (PDF format).

The British Library Online Newspaper Archive (www.uk.olivesoftware.com)

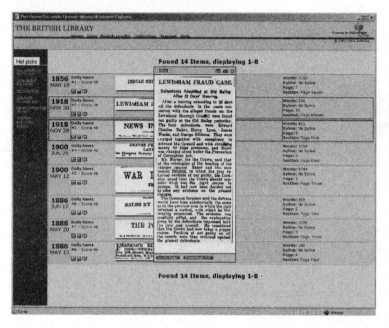

Despite the name, this archive also includes some magazines and books. It is free to search and to view. I do not know if the two of the defendants in this fraud case are my ancestors, but just in case I was glad to see that they were acquitted! This site is well worth a look even if you are not into genealogy.

Old Bailey (www.oldbaileyonline.org)

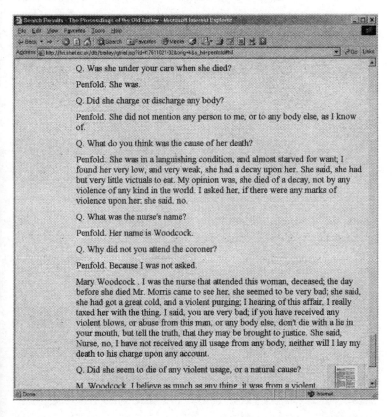

This is an online record of the Old Bailey cases from 1674 to 1834, and fascinating stuff it is too. It seems to be free to search the database and display records of cases. In the extract above, an apothecary called John Penfold is giving evidence in a murder trial in 1761. This is definitely another one that is worth a look even if you are not into genealogy.

Free BMD (http://freebmd.rootsweb.com)

The aim of this site is to put online a record of the birth, marriage, and death certificates for England and Wales from 1837 to 1901. It is not yet complete, and it is perhaps not the easiest of sites to use, but it is a great free recourse. The Free Reg site is a similar facility for parish records from 1538 to 1837. It can be found at:

http://freereg.rootsweb.com

The main Rootsweb site is also worthy of inspection, and is at:

http://rootsweb.com

Family Records Centre
(www.familyrecords.gov.uk)

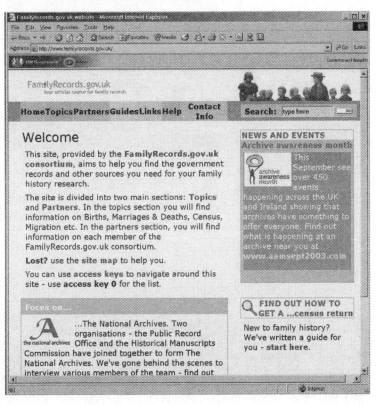

The Family Records Centre is a UK government site that is a guide to the various government departments that hold family records. It is potentially of use to anyone, but it is probably of most use to beginners.

Cyndi's List (www.cyndislist.com)

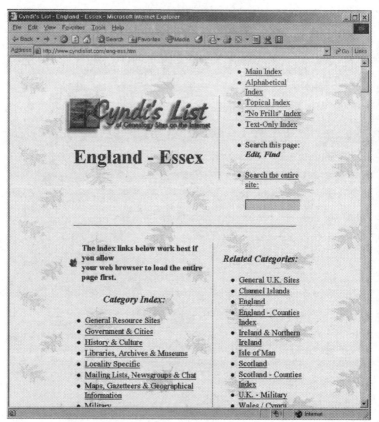

This site is primarily a portal to other genealogy sites, but what a portal. It is claimed that there are more than 193,000 links, and I can well believe it. It includes many useful links for the UK. The site is quite easy to navigate despite its size.

Index

Index

Index